CAROL VORDERMAN
Maths Made Easy

10 Minutes A Day
Fractions

Ages 7-11

DK

Author and Consultant
Sean McArdle

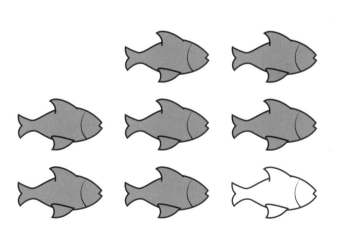

This timer counts up to 10 minutes.
When it reaches 10:00 it will beep.

How to use the timer:
Switch the timer ON.
Press the triangle ▶ to START the timer.
Press the square ■ to STOP or PAUSE the timer.
Press the square ■ to RESET the timer to 00:00.
Press any button to WAKE UP the timer.

 Penguin Random House

Editors Jolyon Goddard, Nishtha Kapil
Art Editor Tanvi Nathyal
Managing Editor Soma B. Chowdhury
Managing Art Editors Richard Czapnik,
Ahlawat Gunjan
Producer, Pre-Production Francesca Wardell
Producer Christine Ni
Math Consultant Sean McArdle
DTP Designer Anita Yadav

First published in Great Britain in 2015 by
Dorling Kindersley Limited
80 Strand, London, WC2R 0RL

A CIP catalogue record for this book
is available from the British Library.
ISBN: 978-0-2411-8232-1

Printed and bound in China.
Timer designed and made in Hong Kong.

All images © Dorling Kindersley Limited
For further information see: www.dkimages.com

A WORLD OF IDEAS:
SEE ALL THERE IS TO KNOW

www.dk.com

Contents

Time taken

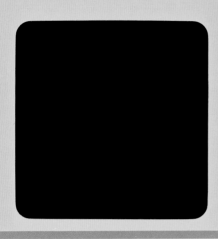

Time filler:
Try writing your own pairs and groups of fractions and then reordering them, starting with either the smallest or the largest fraction. You could also ask a parent to write out sequences with some of the fractions missing and see if you can fill in the missing fractions.

3 Write the fractions in order, starting with the smallest.

$\dfrac{4}{5}$ $\dfrac{1}{5}$ $\dfrac{5}{5}$ ☐ ☐ ☐

$\dfrac{7}{10}$ $\dfrac{3}{10}$ $\dfrac{5}{10}$ ☐ ☐ ☐

$\dfrac{7}{8}$ $\dfrac{4}{8}$ $\dfrac{2}{8}$ ☐ ☐ ☐

$\dfrac{9}{10}$ $\dfrac{6}{10}$ $\dfrac{8}{10}$ ☐ ☐ ☐

4 Write the fractions in order, starting with the largest.

$\dfrac{8}{9}$ $\dfrac{3}{9}$ $\dfrac{5}{9}$ $\dfrac{7}{9}$ ☐ ☐ ☐ ☐

$\dfrac{8}{8}$ $\dfrac{4}{8}$ $\dfrac{2}{8}$ $\dfrac{5}{8}$ ☐ ☐ ☐ ☐

$\dfrac{2}{7}$ $\dfrac{4}{7}$ $\dfrac{1}{7}$ $\dfrac{6}{7}$ ☐ ☐ ☐ ☐

$\dfrac{4}{10}$ $\dfrac{7}{10}$ $\dfrac{5}{10}$ $\dfrac{8}{10}$ ☐ ☐ ☐ ☐

5 Write the fractions in order, starting with the smallest.

$\dfrac{6}{10}$ $\dfrac{2}{10}$ $\dfrac{5}{10}$ $\dfrac{8}{10}$ $\dfrac{7}{10}$ $\dfrac{3}{10}$ ☐ ☐ ☐ ☐ ☐ ☐

Counting in hundredths

Measurements and money involve counting in hundredths, so you will find these exercises really useful.

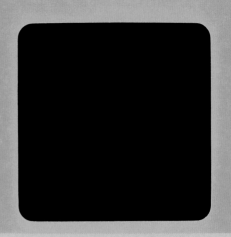

(1) Write each amount as a hundredth of a pound (£).
Note: £1 = 100 pence. $1p = \frac{1}{100} \times £1$

5p   13p   8p   15p

21p   18p   26p   2p

40p   58p   67p   95p

(2) Write each amount as a hundredth of a metre (m).
Note: 1 metre = 100 centimetres. $1cm = \frac{1}{100} \times 1m$

4cm   27cm   53cm   88cm

(3) A new TV costs £300. Paul has saved $\frac{40}{100}$ of the amount. How much more must he save?

Time filler:
Measure the length of different objects on your desk or around the house in centimetres. Then write out each length as a hundredth of a metre. Ask an adult to give you a handful of pennies. Count them and then give the total as hundredths of a pound.

(4) Fill in the missing fractions to complete each sequence.

$\frac{10}{100}$ ⬚ $\frac{30}{100}$ ⬚ ⬚ ⬚ $\frac{70}{100}$ ⬚ ⬚

$\frac{100}{100}$ ⬚ ⬚ ⬚ ⬚ $\frac{50}{100}$ ⬚ ⬚ ⬚ ⬚

(5) A class raises £100 for a Christmas party.
They spend $\frac{60}{100}$ on the party.
The rest they give to charity.
How much do they give to charity?

⬚

(6) How much is one-hundredth ($\frac{1}{100}$) of each amount?

£2 ⬚   3.5 m ⬚   60 m ⬚   10 m ⬚

9 m ⬚   £20 ⬚   £100 ⬚   70 m ⬚

£6 ⬚   £400 ⬚   £19 ⬚   £130 ⬚

Harder fractions

Learning about fractions can be hard work,
but your efforts will be well worth it.
Tackle the problems on these pages and
you will soon discover just how useful
fractions can be in day-to-day life.

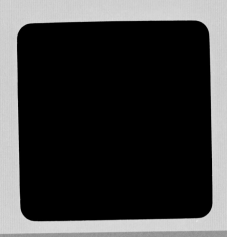

1 Work out five-sixths ($\frac{5}{6}$) of each amount.

18 g ☐   30 cm ☐   60 kg ☐   72 p ☐

2 What is nine-tenths ($\frac{9}{10}$) of each amount?

130 kg ☐   250 g ☐   80 p ☐   10 p ☐

3 How many days are there in five-sevenths ($\frac{5}{7}$) of each period of time?

3 weeks ☐   12 weeks ☐

7 weeks ☐   20 weeks ☐

4 What fraction of the larger number is the smaller number?

6 is $\frac{\square}{\square}$ of 18   5 is $\frac{\square}{\square}$ of 20   18 is $\frac{\square}{\square}$ of 36

5 What fraction of the larger amount is the smaller amount?

3 p and £3 $\frac{\square}{\square}$ 1.5 m and 6 m $\frac{\square}{\square}$

Time filler:
Answer this problem: Sean bought a book for £5.50. He paid with a £10 note. What fraction of the note did he receive as change? Create more of your own problems with fractions and find the answers.

(6) Work out these word problems.

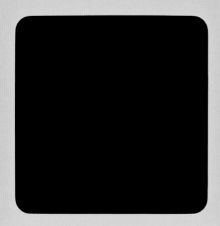

Oliver has 100 toy bricks. $\frac{9}{10}$ of the bricks are red. How many bricks are not red?

[   ] bricks

Katie buys a dozen apples but $\frac{1}{6}$ are rotten. How many apples are not rotten?

[   ] apples

(7) How long is two-thirds ($\frac{2}{3}$) of each lesson? Give your answer in minutes.

The lesson is half-an-hour long.

[   ]

The lesson is 1 hour long.

[   ]

The lesson is $2\frac{1}{2}$ hours long.

[   ]

(8) In each pair, the smaller number is the same fraction of the bigger number. What is the fraction?

32 (28)   64 (56)   40 (35) | 80 (32)   150 (60)   200 (80)

[ ]/[ ]   [ ]/[ ]

Equivalent fractions 2

Here is some more practice at spotting fractions that look totally different but are, in fact, the same. Soon you will be an expert at recognising equivalent fractions!

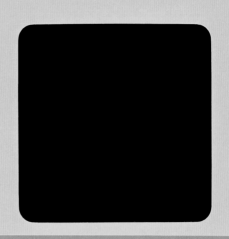

1 Circle the fractions that are equivalent to one-quarter ($\frac{1}{4}$).

$\frac{2}{8}$ $\frac{5}{20}$ $\frac{6}{30}$ $\frac{40}{160}$ $\frac{7}{26}$ $\frac{100}{400}$

2 Circle the fractions that are equivalent to two-fifths ($\frac{2}{5}$).

$\frac{4}{8}$ $\frac{20}{50}$ $\frac{22}{55}$ $\frac{8}{20}$ $\frac{3}{6}$ $\frac{400}{1\,000}$

3 Circle the fractions that are equivalent to seven-tenths ($\frac{7}{10}$).

$\frac{14}{20}$ $\frac{21}{30}$ $\frac{28}{50}$ $\frac{70}{100}$ $\frac{42}{70}$ $\frac{8}{11}$

4 Solve these sums.

What is $\frac{9}{10}$ of £1? ⬚   How long is $\frac{7}{100}$ of 3 m? ⬚

What is $\frac{7}{100}$ of £2? ⬚   How much is $\frac{3}{10}$ of 5 kg? ⬚

5 Fill in the boxes to complete this group of equivalent fractions.

$$\frac{6}{8} = \frac{\square}{72} = \frac{60}{\square} = \frac{\square}{16} = \frac{72}{\square}$$

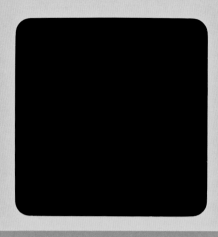

Time filler:
Draw a circle and colour in $\frac{3}{4}$ of it. Now show the coloured part as the equivalent fraction, $\frac{6}{8}$, by drawing more lines on the circle with a ruler. Then show the coloured area as $\frac{12}{16}$ and $\frac{24}{32}$ by drawing even more lines.

---

6 A chessboard is square. It is divided into 64 smaller squares.

How many small squares are there on $\frac{7}{8}$ of the board?  squares

How many small squares are there on $\frac{3}{4}$ of the board? [_____] squares

---

7 Simplify each fraction.

$\frac{20}{30}$ [____]

$\frac{12}{18}$ [____]

$\frac{16}{48}$ [____]

$\frac{70}{100}$ [____]

$\frac{18}{36}$ [____]

$\frac{19}{76}$ [____]

$\frac{72}{96}$ [____]

$\frac{2\,000}{3\,000}$ [____]

---

8 Write four more equivalent fractions for each fraction.

$\frac{3}{5} = \frac{}{} = \frac{}{} = \frac{}{} = \frac{}{}$

$\frac{5}{12} = \frac{}{} = \frac{}{} = \frac{}{} = \frac{}{}$

$\frac{7}{8} = \frac{}{} = \frac{}{} = \frac{}{} = \frac{}{}$

$\frac{9}{10} = \frac{}{} = \frac{}{} = \frac{}{} = \frac{}{}$

Adding fractions 2

Adding fractions together can give you a fraction where the numerator is greater than the denominator. Here, you will practise converting these "improper" fractions to mixed numbers.

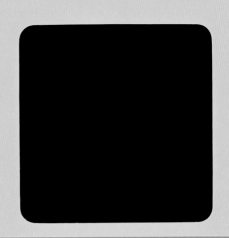

(1) Add the fractions. Then write answers as whole numbers and fractions.

$\frac{1}{2} + \frac{3}{2} = \boxed{} = \boxed{}$
$\frac{3}{2} + \frac{2}{2} = \boxed{} = \boxed{}$
$\frac{5}{2} + \frac{4}{2} = \boxed{} = \boxed{}$

$\frac{4}{2} + \frac{7}{2} = \boxed{} = \boxed{}$
$\frac{1}{4} + \frac{3}{4} = \boxed{} = \boxed{}$
$\frac{6}{4} + \frac{2}{4} = \boxed{} = \boxed{}$

$\frac{4}{4} + \frac{3}{4} = \boxed{} = \boxed{}$
$\frac{6}{4} + \frac{5}{4} = \boxed{} = \boxed{}$
$\frac{2}{4} + \frac{3}{4} = \boxed{} = \boxed{}$

(2) Find the totals.

$\frac{1}{2} + \frac{1}{2} + \frac{1}{2} = \boxed{} = \boxed{}$
$\frac{1}{2} + \frac{1}{2} + \frac{1}{2} + \frac{1}{2} + \frac{1}{2} + \frac{1}{2} + \frac{1}{2} = \boxed{} = \boxed{}$

$\frac{1}{2} + \frac{1}{2} + \frac{1}{2} + \frac{1}{2} + \frac{1}{2} = \boxed{} = \boxed{}$
$\frac{1}{2} + \frac{1}{2} + \frac{1}{2} + \frac{1}{2} + \frac{1}{2} + \frac{1}{2} = \boxed{} = \boxed{}$

(3) How many fifths altogether? Convert answers to a whole number and a fraction.

$\frac{2}{5} + \frac{7}{5} = \boxed{} = \boxed{}$
$\frac{3}{5} + \frac{3}{5} = \boxed{} = \boxed{}$
$\frac{10}{5} + \frac{5}{5} = \boxed{} = \boxed{}$

(4) How many tenths altogether? Convert answers to a whole number and a fraction.

$\frac{7}{10} + \frac{6}{10} = \boxed{} = \boxed{}$
$\frac{8}{10} + \frac{4}{10} = \boxed{} = \boxed{}$

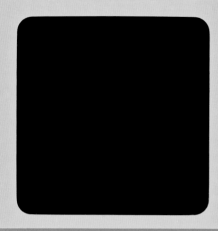

Time filler:
Can you solve this problem?
You are given £3 to spend on a school visit to the zoo. At the gift shop, you buy a notebook for £1.50, a pencil for 60 p and a rubber for 40 p. What fraction of your money do you spend?

---

5 Add $\frac{3}{5}$ to each fraction. Write the answers as mixed numbers.

$\frac{2}{5}$ ☐ $\frac{3}{5}$ ☐ $\frac{5}{5}$ ☐ $\frac{9}{5}$ ☐

---

6 Add $\frac{7}{10}$ to each fraction. Write the answers as mixed numbers.

$\frac{7}{10}$ ☐ $\frac{3}{10}$ ☐ $\frac{9}{10}$ ☐ $\frac{4}{10}$ ☐

---

7 What must be added to $\frac{2}{5}$ to make $\frac{4}{5}$? ☐

8 What is the total of $\frac{2}{3}$, $\frac{3}{3}$ and $\frac{4}{3}$? ☐

---

9 A class has 30 children.

$\frac{3}{5}$ of them are boys. What fraction are the girls? ☐

$\frac{1}{4}$ of them have green eyes. What fraction do not have green eyes? ☐

3 children were born in March. What fraction of the class is that? ☐

Subtracting fractions 2

Try these fraction subtractions. This time, however, check to see if any of your answers can be simplified. That is, whether an answer can be written as an equivalent fraction using numbers of lower value for the numerator and denominator.

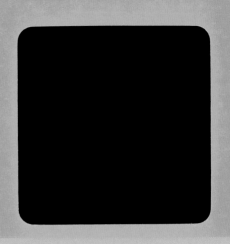

(1) Write the answers. Simplify any answers you can.

$\frac{7}{3} - \frac{2}{3} =$ ☐

$\frac{12}{6} - \frac{9}{6} =$ ☐

$\frac{9}{10} - \frac{9}{10} =$ ☐

$\frac{9}{3} - \frac{6}{3} =$ ☐

$\frac{10}{6} - \frac{4}{6} =$ ☐

$\frac{18}{15} - \frac{12}{15} =$ ☐

$\frac{5}{6} - \frac{3}{6} =$ ☐

$\frac{10}{3} - \frac{3}{3} =$ ☐

$\frac{12}{10} - \frac{11}{10} =$ ☐

$\frac{9}{7} - \frac{2}{7} =$ ☐

$\frac{15}{6} - \frac{11}{6} =$ ☐

$\frac{20}{10} - \frac{18}{10} =$ ☐

$\frac{5}{6} - \frac{5}{6} =$ ☐

$\frac{12}{3} - \frac{10}{3} =$ ☐

$\frac{9}{10} - \frac{4}{10} =$ ☐

$\frac{7}{8} - \frac{4}{8} =$ ☐

$\frac{5}{12} - \frac{4}{12} =$ ☐

$\frac{17}{10} - \frac{12}{10} =$ ☐

$\frac{7}{9} - \frac{2}{9} =$ ☐

$\frac{7}{20} - \frac{3}{20} =$ ☐

$\frac{12}{10} - \frac{2}{10} =$ ☐

(2) Subtract $\frac{3}{5}$ from each fraction.

$\frac{8}{5}$ ☐

$\frac{12}{5}$ ☐

$\frac{22}{5}$ ☐

$\frac{31}{5}$ ☐

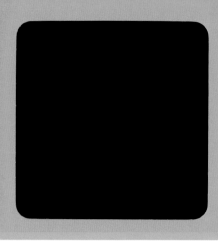

Time filler:
Mary has £10 in her purse. On a visit to the seaside, she spends $\frac{2}{5}$ of it on ice cream for her family. She also spends another $\frac{1}{5}$ on a carton of orange juice. What fraction of money is Mary left with? How much money is this?

---

3 What fraction is $\frac{7}{8}$ less than each of these?

$\frac{8}{8}$ ⬚

$\frac{12}{8}$ ⬚

$\frac{20}{8}$ ⬚

$\frac{32}{8}$ ⬚

---

4 Continue each sequence.

$\frac{20}{3}$ $\quad$ $\frac{17}{3}$ $\quad$ $\frac{14}{3}$ $\quad$ $\frac{11}{3}$ $\quad$ ⬚ $\quad$ ⬚

$\frac{18}{20}$ $\quad$ $\frac{16}{20}$ $\quad$ $\frac{14}{20}$ $\quad$ $\frac{12}{20}$ $\quad$ ⬚ $\quad$ ⬚

---

5 What fraction is ...

... $\frac{3}{5}$ less than $\frac{6}{5}$? ⬚

... $\frac{7}{10}$ less than $\frac{15}{10}$? ⬚

... $\frac{9}{6}$ less than $\frac{12}{6}$?  ⬚

... $\frac{1}{2}$ less than $\frac{21}{2}$? ⬚

---

6 In a swimming class, $\frac{1}{10}$ of the students can do the breaststroke, $\frac{6}{10}$ can do the crawl and $\frac{2}{10}$ can do the butterfly stroke. The remaining students cannot swim. What fraction of the class cannot swim? ⬚

Comparing, ordering and simplifying

Sharpen your skill at sizing up fractions.
Remember that finding a common denominator
is the key to comparing the size of fractions.

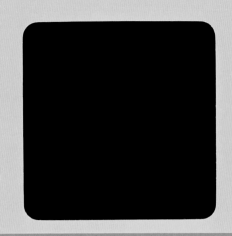

1 Write the fractions in order, starting with the smallest.

$\frac{1}{2}$ $\frac{2}{8}$ $\frac{3}{4}$ ☐ ☐ ☐ $\frac{4}{3}$ $\frac{9}{12}$ $\frac{3}{6}$ ☐ ☐ ☐

$\frac{3}{8}$ $\frac{5}{2}$ $\frac{2}{4}$ ☐ ☐ ☐ $\frac{4}{5}$ $\frac{9}{10}$ $\frac{7}{10}$ ☐ ☐ ☐

2 Simplify each fraction to a whole number.

$\frac{12}{6}$ ☐ $\frac{9}{3}$ ☐ $\frac{16}{2}$ ☐ $\frac{20}{10}$ ☐

$\frac{16}{4}$ ☐ $\frac{12}{3}$ ☐ $\frac{14}{7}$ ☐ $\frac{24}{6}$ ☐

$\frac{8}{2}$ ☐ $\frac{24}{2}$ ☐ $\frac{12}{2}$ ☐ $\frac{50}{2}$ ☐

$\frac{72}{4}$ ☐ $\frac{60}{5}$ ☐ $\frac{80}{4}$ ☐ $\frac{100}{5}$ ☐

$\frac{24}{3}$ ☐ $\frac{30}{6}$ ☐ $\frac{42}{7}$ ☐ $\frac{200}{10}$ ☐

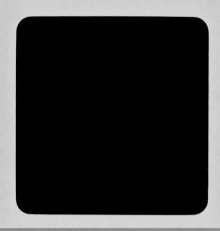

Time filler:

Write these fractions in order, starting with the smallest: $\frac{2}{3}$ $\frac{1}{4}$ $\frac{7}{30}$ $\frac{5}{6}$ $\frac{8}{15}$ $\frac{17}{60}$

Now write these mixed numbers in order, starting with the largest: $1\frac{3}{5}$ $2\frac{1}{12}$ $3\frac{1}{3}$ $1\frac{5}{8}$ $1\frac{1}{3}$

---

3 Circle the larger fraction in each pair.

$\frac{12}{4}$ $\frac{4}{2}$ 　　　　$\frac{18}{6}$ $\frac{12}{3}$ 　　　　$\frac{30}{10}$ $\frac{50}{5}$ 　　　　$\frac{48}{12}$ $\frac{20}{4}$

---

4 Circle the smallest fraction in each group.

$\frac{5}{2}$ $\frac{8}{12}$ $\frac{2}{6}$ 　　　$\frac{9}{4}$ $\frac{12}{8}$ $\frac{5}{2}$ 　　　$\frac{3}{5}$ $\frac{12}{10}$ $\frac{1}{20}$ 　　　$\frac{7}{8}$ $\frac{2}{4}$ $\frac{3}{8}$

---

5 Write each fraction as a mixed number.

$\frac{3}{2}$ = □ $\frac{□}{□}$ 　　　　$\frac{13}{4}$ = □ $\frac{□}{□}$ 　　　　$\frac{8}{5}$ = □ $\frac{□}{□}$

$\frac{7}{2}$ = □ $\frac{□}{□}$ 　　　　$\frac{15}{2}$ = □ $\frac{□}{□}$ 　　　　$\frac{27}{4}$ = □ $\frac{□}{□}$

$\frac{19}{3}$ = □ $\frac{□}{□}$ 　　　　$\frac{38}{5}$ = □ $\frac{□}{□}$ 　　　　$\frac{51}{7}$ = □ $\frac{□}{□}$

Mixed numbers and improper fractions

You have now practised plenty of top-heavy (improper) fractions. Here is some practice at converting them to mixed numbers.

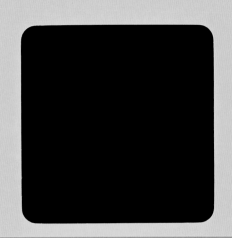

① Convert each mixed number to an improper fraction.

$3\frac{1}{2} = \dfrac{\Box}{\Box}$ $5\frac{1}{3} = \dfrac{\Box}{\Box}$ $7\frac{7}{10} = \dfrac{\Box}{\Box}$ $7\frac{2}{5} = \dfrac{\Box}{\Box}$

$3\frac{1}{10} = \dfrac{\Box}{\Box}$ $5\frac{1}{2} = \dfrac{\Box}{\Box}$ $8\frac{7}{8} = \dfrac{\Box}{\Box}$ $6\frac{2}{5} = \dfrac{\Box}{\Box}$

$8\frac{7}{10} = \dfrac{\Box}{\Box}$ $4\frac{5}{6} = \dfrac{\Box}{\Box}$ $3\frac{9}{10} = \dfrac{\Box}{\Box}$ $3\frac{3}{8} = \dfrac{\Box}{\Box}$

$1\frac{1}{10} = \dfrac{\Box}{\Box}$ $4\frac{4}{5} = \dfrac{\Box}{\Box}$ $2\frac{7}{9} = \dfrac{\Box}{\Box}$ $10\frac{5}{6} = \dfrac{\Box}{\Box}$

$10\frac{3}{4} = \dfrac{\Box}{\Box}$ $5\frac{1}{8} = \dfrac{\Box}{\Box}$ $6\frac{3}{5} = \dfrac{\Box}{\Box}$ $12\frac{1}{2} = \dfrac{\Box}{\Box}$

$11\frac{4}{7} = \dfrac{\Box}{\Box}$ $5\frac{3}{4} = \dfrac{\Box}{\Box}$ $2\frac{3}{5} = \dfrac{\Box}{\Box}$ $6\frac{5}{8} = \dfrac{\Box}{\Box}$

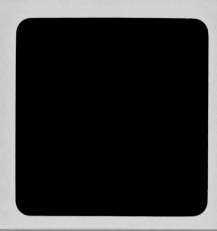

Time filler:
Write out your own list of improper fractions and then convert each of them to a mixed number. Then write out a list of mixed numbers and convert each one into an improper fraction.

(2) Write each improper fraction as a mixed number.

$\frac{14}{3}$ ☐ $\frac{\square}{\square}$

$\frac{27}{2}$ ☐ $\frac{\square}{\square}$

$\frac{16}{5}$ ☐ $\frac{\square}{\square}$

$\frac{26}{10}$ ☐ $\frac{\square}{\square}$

$\frac{19}{4}$ ☐ $\frac{\square}{\square}$

$\frac{12}{10}$ ☐ $\frac{\square}{\square}$

$\frac{13}{3}$ ☐ $\frac{\square}{\square}$

$\frac{32}{10}$ ☐ $\frac{\square}{\square}$

$\frac{15}{9}$ ☐ $\frac{\square}{\square}$

$\frac{13}{12}$ ☐ $\frac{\square}{\square}$

$\frac{42}{10}$ ☐ $\frac{\square}{\square}$

$\frac{81}{2}$ ☐ $\frac{\square}{\square}$

$\frac{29}{4}$ ☐ $\frac{\square}{\square}$

$\frac{62}{5}$ ☐ $\frac{\square}{\square}$

$\frac{67}{11}$ ☐ $\frac{\square}{\square}$

$\frac{39}{12}$ ☐ $\frac{\square}{\square}$

$\frac{30}{7}$ ☐ $\frac{\square}{\square}$

$\frac{50}{20}$ ☐ $\frac{\square}{\square}$

Adding, subtracting and simplifying

Consolidate what you have learned so far!
You will soon be quite an expert at handling
fractions. Check carefully for accuracy.

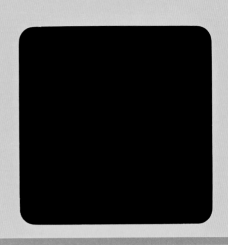

1 Write the answers as mixed numbers.

$$\frac{2}{3} + \frac{2}{3} = \square \frac{\square}{\square}$$

$$\frac{3}{4} + \frac{2}{4} = \square \frac{\square}{\square}$$

$$\frac{4}{5} + \frac{4}{5} = \square \frac{\square}{\square}$$

$$\frac{6}{7} + \frac{4}{7} = \square \frac{\square}{\square}$$

$$\frac{5}{6} + \frac{4}{6} = \square \frac{\square}{\square}$$

$$\frac{7}{8} + \frac{3}{8} = \square \frac{\square}{\square}$$

$$\frac{9}{10} + \frac{3}{10} = \square \frac{\square}{\square}$$

$$\frac{7}{10} + \frac{6}{10} = \square \frac{\square}{\square}$$

$$\frac{9}{15} + \frac{16}{15} = \square \frac{\square}{\square}$$

2 Do the subtraction and simplify the answer.

$$\frac{9}{10} - \frac{4}{10} = \frac{\square}{\square} = \frac{\square}{\square}$$

$$\frac{7}{15} - \frac{4}{15} = \frac{\square}{\square} = \frac{\square}{\square}$$

$$\frac{20}{25} - \frac{5}{25} = \frac{\square}{\square} = \frac{\square}{\square}$$

$$\frac{17}{30} - \frac{9}{30} = \frac{\square}{\square} = \frac{\square}{\square}$$

$$\frac{11}{20} - \frac{6}{20} = \frac{\square}{\square} = \frac{\square}{\square}$$

$$\frac{8}{15} - \frac{3}{15} = \frac{\square}{\square} = \frac{\square}{\square}$$

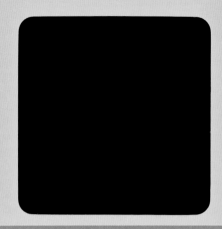

(3) Write the answers as mixed numbers.

$2\frac{3}{5} + 4\frac{1}{5} = \bigcirc \frac{\square}{\square}$

$3\frac{1}{4} + 4\frac{1}{4} = \bigcirc \frac{\square}{\square}$

$3\frac{3}{10} + 4\frac{1}{10} = \bigcirc \frac{\square}{\square}$

$8\frac{2}{5} + 3\frac{4}{5} = \bigcirc \frac{\square}{\square}$

$6\frac{1}{4} + 2\frac{1}{4} + 4\frac{1}{4} = \bigcirc \frac{\square}{\square}$

$12\frac{1}{2} + 3\frac{1}{2} + 4\frac{1}{2} = \bigcirc \frac{\square}{\square}$

(4) Write the answers as mixed numbers.

$6 - 3\frac{3}{4} = \bigcirc \frac{\square}{\square}$ $2\frac{2}{3} - 1 = \bigcirc \frac{\square}{\square}$ $7 - 1\frac{4}{5} = \bigcirc \frac{\square}{\square}$

$4 - 1\frac{1}{3} = \bigcirc \frac{\square}{\square}$ $5\frac{1}{2} - 3 = \bigcirc \frac{\square}{\square}$ $6 - 1\frac{2}{10} = \bigcirc \frac{\square}{\square}$

$7 - 1\frac{1}{6} = \bigcirc \frac{\square}{\square}$ $3\frac{1}{2} - 2 = \bigcirc \frac{\square}{\square}$ $8 - 6\frac{1}{4} = \bigcirc \frac{\square}{\square}$

Beat the clock 2

Now test your improved fraction skills.
Work quickly, but remember it is important to
check all the answers. How many sums can you
do in 10 minutes?

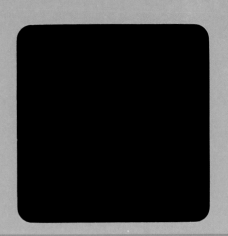

Convert each mixed number to an improper fraction.

(1) $3\frac{1}{2}$

(2) $7\frac{1}{3}$

(3) $2\frac{9}{10}$

(4) $4\frac{4}{7}$

(5) $8\frac{2}{3}$

(6) $4\frac{3}{12}$

(7) $4\frac{1}{5}$

(8) $8\frac{2}{5}$

(9) $10\frac{3}{5}$

(10) $6\frac{4}{7}$

(11) $6\frac{6}{9}$

(12) $10\frac{1}{5}$

(13) $4\frac{5}{9}$

(14) $9\frac{7}{9}$

(15) $20\frac{5}{6}$

Convert each improper fraction to a mixed number.

(16) $\frac{43}{12}$

(17) $\frac{18}{5}$

(18) $\frac{21}{2}$

(19) $\frac{33}{10}$

(20) $\frac{14}{3}$

(21) $\frac{50}{8}$

(22) $\frac{43}{6}$

(23) $\frac{73}{12}$

(24) $\frac{55}{9}$

Write each fraction in its simplest form.

(25) $\frac{4}{8}$

(26) $\frac{12}{18}$

(27) $\frac{30}{40}$

(28) $\frac{16}{20}$

(29) $\frac{18}{20}$

(30) $\frac{15}{25}$

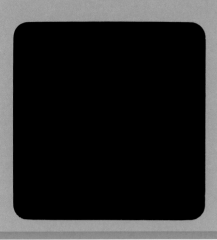

Convert each improper fraction to a whole number.

(31) $\frac{36}{3}$

(32) $\frac{45}{9}$

(33) $\frac{88}{11}$

(34) $\frac{63}{9}$

(35) $\frac{28}{7}$

(36) $\frac{72}{12}$

(37) $\frac{108}{12}$

(38) $\frac{200}{5}$

(39) $\frac{1\,000}{10}$

Add the fractions. Simplify answers or convert them to a mixed or whole number.

(40) $\frac{1}{2}+\frac{2}{2}+\frac{3}{2}=\boxed{}=\boxed{}$

(41) $\frac{1}{3}+\frac{2}{3}+\frac{3}{3}=\boxed{}=\boxed{}$

(42) $\frac{1}{5}+\frac{2}{5}+\frac{3}{5}=\boxed{}=\boxed{}$

(43) $\frac{1}{10}+\frac{2}{10}+\frac{3}{10}=\boxed{}=\boxed{}$

(44) $2\frac{2}{5}+3\frac{2}{5}+4\frac{2}{5}=\boxed{}=\boxed{}$

(45) $2\frac{1}{2}+3\frac{1}{2}+4\frac{1}{2}=\boxed{}=\boxed{}$

Circle the smaller fraction in each pair.

(46) $1\frac{1}{4}$ $\qquad$ $\frac{3}{4}$

(47) $1\frac{7}{8}$ $\qquad$ $\frac{14}{8}$

(48) $3\frac{2}{3}$ $\qquad$ $\frac{10}{3}$

(49) $2\frac{5}{9}$ $\qquad$ $\frac{24}{9}$

(50) $7\frac{3}{4}$ $\qquad$ $\frac{19}{4}$

(51) $10\frac{7}{10}$ $\qquad$ $\frac{90}{10}$

(52) $10\frac{1}{12}$ $\qquad$ $\frac{120}{12}$

(53) $1\frac{2}{9}$ $\qquad$ $\frac{12}{9}$

(54) $\frac{20}{6}$ $\qquad$ $3\frac{5}{6}$

Multiplying fractions 1

Make sure that you really know your times tables before you attempt to work out the sums on these pages.

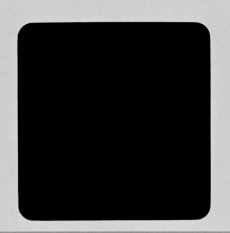

1 Multiply each fraction by 4.

$\frac{1}{2}$ ☐ $\frac{1}{4}$ ☐ $\frac{1}{5}$ ☐ $\frac{1}{10}$ ☐

2 Multiply each fraction by 7.

$\frac{1}{2}$ ☐ $\frac{1}{3}$ ☐ $\frac{1}{10}$ ☐ $\frac{1}{4}$ ☐

3 Multiply each fraction by 10.

$\frac{1}{2}$ ☐ $\frac{1}{5}$ ☐ $\frac{1}{4}$ ☐ $\frac{1}{6}$ ☐

4 Multiply each fraction by 6.

$\frac{1}{6}$ ☐ $\frac{1}{4}$ ☐ $\frac{1}{10}$ ☐ $\frac{1}{12}$ ☐

5 Multiply each number by $\frac{1}{2}$.

6 ☐   12 ☐   1 ☐   20 ☐

6 Multiply each number by $\frac{1}{4}$.

12 ☐   24 ☐   40 ☐   100 ☐

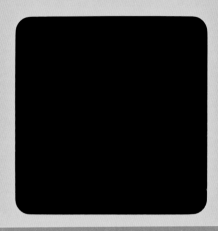

Time filler:
Tom invites 12 friends to his birthday party. He serves pizza. Out of Tom's guests, 7 eat half a pizza each. Everyone else at the party eats $\frac{1}{4}$ of a pizza each. How many pizzas get eaten altogether?

7) Multiply each number by $\frac{1}{5}$ and write the answer as an improper fraction and then as a mixed number.

6 ☐ = ☐   18 ☐ = ☐   24 ☐ = ☐

8) Multiply each number by $\frac{1}{10}$ and write the answer as an improper fraction and then as a mixed number.

15 ☐ = ☐   24 ☐ = ☐   45 ☐ = ☐

9) Multiply each fraction by 7 and write the answer as an improper fraction and then as a mixed number.

$\frac{1}{3}$ ☐ = ☐ $\frac{1}{4}$ ☐ = ☐ $\frac{1}{5}$ ☐ = ☐

10) Mrs Brown buys some lemonade for a school picnic. Ten children drink a quarter of a bottle each. How many bottles do the children drink altogether? Give your answer as a mixed number.

☐

Multiplying fractions 2

Here are some slightly harder
multiplication sums for you to tackle.
Good luck!

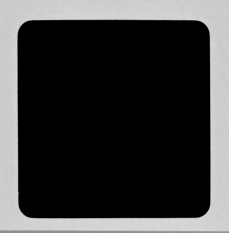

(1) Multiply each fraction by 8 and write the answer as an improper
fraction and then as a mixed number.

$\frac{1}{3}$ ⬚ = ⬚ $\frac{3}{7}$ ⬚ = ⬚ $\frac{4}{5}$ ⬚ = ⬚

(2) Multiply each fraction by 4 and write the answer as an improper
fraction and then as a mixed number.

$\frac{2}{5}$ ⬚ = ⬚ $\frac{2}{3}$ ⬚ = ⬚ $\frac{3}{5}$ ⬚ = ⬚

(3) Multiply each fraction by 6 and write the answer as an improper
fraction and then as a mixed number.

$\frac{3}{4}$ ⬚ = ⬚ $\frac{4}{5}$ ⬚ = ⬚ $\frac{2}{7}$ ⬚ = ⬚

(4) Multiply each fraction by 12 and write the answer as an improper
fraction and then as a mixed number.

$\frac{3}{7}$ ⬚ = ⬚ $\frac{2}{5}$ ⬚ = ⬚ $\frac{6}{10}$ ⬚ = ⬚

(5) Multiply each fraction by 10 and write the answer as an improper
fraction and then as a mixed number.

$\frac{7}{12}$ ⬚ = ⬚ $\frac{4}{3}$ ⬚ = ⬚ $\frac{5}{6}$ ⬚ = ⬚

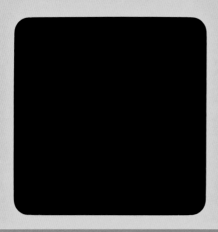

Time filler:
Sue takes the bus to and from school every day. Each single journey costs her $\frac{1}{20}$ of her weekly pocket money. What fraction of her pocket money does Sue spend each week on bus fares?

6 Multiply each number by $\frac{1}{4}$ and simplify the answer.

24 ☐ = ☐   40 ☐ = ☐   32 ☐ = ☐

7 Multiply each number by $\frac{3}{5}$ and write the answer as an improper fraction and then as a mixed number.

12 ☐ = ☐   16 ☐ = ☐   21 ☐ = ☐

8 Multiply each number by $\frac{3}{4}$ and write the answer as an improper fraction and then as a mixed number.

15 ☐ = ☐   21 ☐ = ☐   26 ☐ = ☐

9 Multiply each fraction by 9 and write the answer as an improper fraction and then as a mixed number.

$\frac{2}{7}$ ☐ = ☐ $\frac{3}{4}$ ☐ = ☐ $\frac{4}{5}$ ☐ = ☐

10 Multiply each fraction by 11 and write the answer as an improper fraction and then as a mixed number.

$\frac{3}{4}$ ☐ = ☐ $\frac{5}{7}$ ☐ = ☐ $\frac{3}{8}$ ☐ = ☐

Multiplying and simplifying

Look out for fractions that can be simplified before you multiply them. It should make the calculation easier.

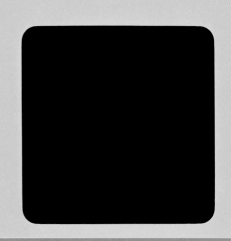

1 Multiply the fractions.

$\frac{1}{2} \times \frac{1}{3} =$ ☐

$\frac{1}{2} \times \frac{1}{4} =$ ☐

$\frac{1}{5} \times \frac{1}{2} =$ ☐

$\frac{1}{10} \times \frac{1}{2} =$ ☐

$\frac{1}{5} \times \frac{2}{3} =$ ☐

$\frac{3}{4} \times \frac{1}{2} =$ ☐

2 Multiply the fractions and simplify the answers.

$\frac{6}{10} \times \frac{2}{3} =$ ☐

$\frac{3}{5} \times \frac{5}{8} =$ ☐

$\frac{3}{4} \times \frac{5}{6} =$ ☐

$\frac{1}{4} \times \frac{2}{3} =$ ☐

$\frac{1}{4} \times \frac{4}{7} =$ ☐

$\frac{3}{10} \times \frac{5}{7} =$ ☐

$\frac{1}{3} \times \frac{3}{5} =$ ☐

$\frac{3}{8} \times \frac{2}{3} =$ ☐

$\frac{1}{10} \times \frac{2}{3} =$ ☐

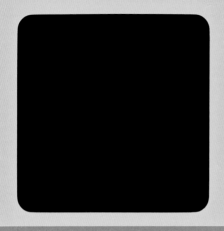

Time filler:

Give the answers in their simplest form:

$\frac{2}{3} \times \frac{3}{10}$ 　　　　 $\frac{1}{5} \times \frac{3}{4}$ 　　　　 $\frac{1}{7} \times \frac{7}{8}$

$\frac{3}{8} \times \frac{1}{4} \times \frac{1}{6}$ 　　　 $\frac{1}{6} \times \frac{1}{8} \times \frac{3}{8}$ 　　　 $\frac{2}{5} \times \frac{1}{3} \times \frac{5}{12}$

---

3 Multiply the fractions. Write the answer in its simplest form.

$\frac{1}{10} \times \frac{1}{5} = \boxed{}$ 　　　 $\frac{2}{5} \times \frac{2}{10} = \boxed{}$ 　　　 $\frac{1}{12} \times \frac{2}{3} = \boxed{}$

$\frac{2}{12} \times \frac{3}{4} = \boxed{}$ 　　　 $\frac{3}{12} \times \frac{3}{4} = \boxed{}$ 　　　 $\frac{5}{12} \times \frac{2}{3} = \boxed{}$

$\frac{6}{12} \times \frac{5}{10} = \boxed{}$ 　　　 $\frac{3}{4} \times \frac{6}{8} = \boxed{}$ 　　　 $\frac{1}{2} \times \frac{1}{3} \times \frac{1}{4} = \boxed{}$

$\frac{1}{3} \times \frac{1}{5} \times \frac{1}{10} = \boxed{}$ 　　 $\frac{1}{4} \times \frac{1}{2} \times \frac{3}{4} = \boxed{}$ 　　 $\frac{1}{3} \times \frac{2}{3} \times \frac{1}{4} = \boxed{}$

$\frac{1}{5} \times \frac{1}{3} \times \frac{1}{10} = \boxed{}$ 　　 $\frac{1}{5} \times \frac{2}{3} \times \frac{1}{10} = \boxed{}$ 　　 $\frac{1}{5} \times \frac{2}{5} \times \frac{3}{5} = \boxed{}$

$\frac{1}{4} \times \frac{2}{4} \times \frac{3}{4} = \boxed{}$ 　　 $\frac{7}{12} \times \frac{1}{2} \times \frac{8}{10} = \boxed{}$ 　　 $\frac{3}{4} \times \frac{4}{5} \times \frac{5}{6} = \boxed{}$

Dividing fractions

Now let us practise dividing fractions.
Do not forget to simplify your answers
wherever possible.

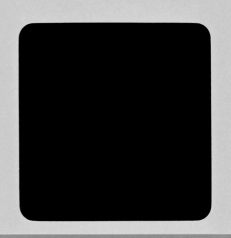

(1) Divide the fractions by the whole numbers. Simplify any answers you can.

$\frac{1}{3} \div 2 =$ ☐

$\frac{1}{4} \div 3 =$ ☐

$\frac{1}{5} \div 2 =$ ☐

$\frac{1}{10} \div 4 =$ ☐

$\frac{2}{3} \div 2 =$ ☐

$\frac{3}{4} \div 2 =$ ☐

$\frac{3}{5} \div 3 =$ ☐

$\frac{1}{10} \div 3 =$ ☐

$\frac{1}{2} \div 10 =$ ☐

$\frac{1}{3} \div 8 =$ ☐

$\frac{1}{10} \div 7 =$ ☐

$\frac{2}{3} \div 4 =$ ☐

$\frac{4}{5} \div 3 =$ ☐

$\frac{3}{4} \div 6 =$ ☐

$\frac{5}{8} \div 10 =$ ☐

$\frac{4}{5} \div 4 =$ ☐

$\frac{2}{3} \div 12 =$ ☐

$\frac{5}{6} \div 10 =$ ☐

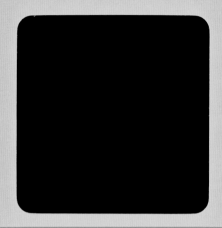

② Write down the answers in their simplest form.

$\frac{4}{9} \div 8 =$ ☐

$\frac{7}{8} \div 7 =$ ☐

$\frac{8}{9} \div 4 =$ ☐

$\frac{5}{7} \div 5 =$ ☐

$\frac{4}{10} \div 4 =$ ☐

$\frac{5}{9} \div 10 =$ ☐

$\frac{6}{7} \div 12 =$ ☐

$\frac{4}{5} \div 12 =$ ☐

$\frac{8}{12} \div 8 =$ ☐

$\frac{3}{7} \div 12 =$ ☐

$\frac{6}{10} \div 4 =$ ☐

$\frac{6}{7} \div 10 =$ ☐

③ Pete has £10. He gives four-fifths $(\frac{4}{5})$ of it to his four children to share equally between them on rides at a fun fair. How much does each child have to spend?

☐

Multiplying and dividing fractions

When you work your way through these pages, you will become an expert at multiplying and dividing fractions.

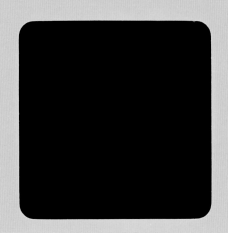

---

(1) Multiply each fraction by 8. Write the answer as an improper fraction and then as a mixed number.

$\frac{4}{7}$ ⬚ = ⬚ $\frac{8}{9}$ ⬚ = ⬚ $\frac{4}{11}$ ⬚ = ⬚

---

(2) Multiply each fraction by 15. Write the answer as an improper fraction and then as a mixed or whole number.

$\frac{1}{4}$ ⬚ = ⬚ $\frac{2}{10}$ ⬚ = ⬚ $\frac{4}{5}$ ⬚ = ⬚

---

(3) Multiply each fraction by 20. Write the answer as an improper fraction and then as a mixed number.

$\frac{5}{6}$ ⬚ = ⬚ $\frac{8}{12}$ ⬚ = ⬚ $\frac{6}{7}$ ⬚ = ⬚

---

(4) Multiply each mixed number by 4. Simplify any answers you can.

$4\frac{1}{8}$ ⬚ $2\frac{1}{4}$ ⬚ $3\frac{3}{4}$ ⬚ $1\frac{1}{2}$ ⬚

---

(5) Multiply each mixed number by 10. Simplify any answers you can.

$4\frac{1}{2}$ ⬚ $5\frac{2}{5}$ ⬚ $7\frac{1}{4}$ ⬚ $10\frac{1}{10}$ ⬚

Time filler:
You decide to bake a lemon cake and find a recipe that serves 8, containing 240 g flour and 120 g butter. You want to serve 6 people. How many grams of flour and butter do you need to make a lemon cake for 6 people?

6 Divide each whole number by 3 and write the answer as a mixed number.

10 ⬚   14 ⬚   20 ⬚   28 ⬚

7 Divide each whole number by 5 and write the answer as a mixed number.

18 ⬚   27 ⬚   43 ⬚   61 ⬚

8 Divide each whole number by 7 and write the answer as a mixed number.

9 ⬚   18 ⬚   45 ⬚   67 ⬚

9 Divide each whole number by 8 and write the answer as a mixed number.

23 ⬚   41 ⬚   9 ⬚   45 ⬚

10 Divide each whole number by 10 and write the answer as a mixed number.

15 ⬚   23 ⬚   56 ⬚   77 ⬚

Common denominators

Use your knowledge of times tables to help find common denominators for pairs and groups of fractions.

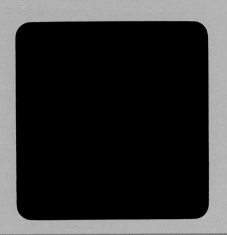

1 Rewrite each pair of fractions so they have the same denominator.

$\dfrac{1}{2}$ $\dfrac{1}{3}$ $\dfrac{}{}$ $\dfrac{}{}$

$\dfrac{1}{4}$ $\dfrac{1}{7}$ $\dfrac{}{}$ $\dfrac{}{}$

$\dfrac{1}{4}$ $\dfrac{1}{2}$ $\dfrac{}{}$ $\dfrac{}{}$

$\dfrac{1}{4}$ $\dfrac{1}{5}$ $\dfrac{}{}$ $\dfrac{}{}$

$\dfrac{1}{6}$ $\dfrac{1}{12}$ $\dfrac{}{}$ $\dfrac{}{}$

$\dfrac{1}{8}$ $\dfrac{1}{9}$ $\dfrac{}{}$ $\dfrac{}{}$

$\dfrac{1}{5}$ $\dfrac{1}{10}$ $\dfrac{}{}$ $\dfrac{}{}$

$\dfrac{1}{4}$ $\dfrac{1}{12}$ $\dfrac{}{}$ $\dfrac{}{}$

$\dfrac{2}{3}$ $\dfrac{1}{2}$ $\dfrac{}{}$ $\dfrac{}{}$

$\dfrac{3}{4}$ $\dfrac{1}{2}$ $\dfrac{}{}$ $\dfrac{}{}$

$\dfrac{2}{5}$ $\dfrac{1}{3}$ $\dfrac{}{}$ $\dfrac{}{}$

$\dfrac{3}{4}$ $\dfrac{1}{5}$ $\dfrac{}{}$ $\dfrac{}{}$

$\dfrac{2}{3}$ $\dfrac{1}{10}$ $\dfrac{}{}$ $\dfrac{}{}$

$\dfrac{3}{4}$ $\dfrac{1}{10}$ $\dfrac{}{}$ $\dfrac{}{}$

$\dfrac{1}{5}$ $\dfrac{3}{10}$ $\dfrac{}{}$ $\dfrac{}{}$

$\dfrac{1}{2}$ $\dfrac{3}{5}$ $\dfrac{}{}$ $\dfrac{}{}$

$\dfrac{1}{10}$ $\dfrac{1}{100}$ $\dfrac{}{}$ $\dfrac{}{}$

$\dfrac{1}{10}$ $\dfrac{1}{1\,000}$ $\dfrac{}{}$ $\dfrac{}{}$

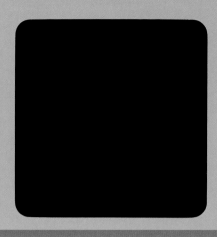

Time filler:
Helen and Kerry buy a bag of sweets to share. Helen eats $\frac{1}{4}$ of the sweets and Kerry eats $\frac{3}{8}$. What fraction of the bag of sweets do they eat altogether? Later, they share a third of the remaining sweets between them. What fraction of the bag of sweets has now been eaten?

(2) Rewrite each group of fractions so they have the same denominator.

$\frac{1}{2}$ $\frac{1}{5}$ $\frac{1}{3}$ ⬚ ⬚ ⬚

$\frac{1}{5}$ $\frac{1}{10}$ $\frac{1}{2}$ ⬚ ⬚ ⬚

$\frac{1}{2}$ $\frac{2}{3}$ $\frac{1}{4}$ ⬚ ⬚ ⬚

$\frac{1}{2}$ $\frac{3}{4}$ $\frac{1}{5}$ ⬚ ⬚ ⬚

$\frac{2}{3}$ $\frac{3}{4}$ $\frac{1}{2}$ ⬚ ⬚ ⬚

$\frac{3}{4}$ $\frac{3}{5}$ $\frac{1}{10}$ ⬚ ⬚ ⬚

$\frac{2}{5}$ $\frac{3}{10}$ $\frac{3}{5}$ ⬚ ⬚ ⬚

$\frac{1}{4}$ $\frac{3}{4}$ $\frac{7}{8}$ ⬚ ⬚ ⬚

$\frac{1}{2}$ $\frac{1}{10}$ $\frac{3}{5}$ ⬚ ⬚ ⬚

$\frac{3}{4}$ $\frac{1}{2}$ $\frac{7}{10}$ ⬚ ⬚ ⬚

$\frac{2}{5}$ $\frac{1}{10}$ $\frac{1}{100}$ ⬚ ⬚ ⬚

$\frac{1}{5}$ $\frac{1}{100}$ $\frac{5}{10}$ ⬚ ⬚ ⬚

Comparing fractions

Remember that comparing the size of different fractions is easy once you have worked out their common denominator.

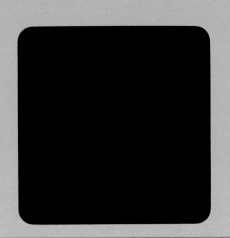

(1) Circle the larger number in each pair.

$\frac{1}{3}$	$\frac{3}{5}$	$\frac{2}{3}$	$\frac{3}{4}$	$\frac{7}{10}$	$\frac{4}{6}$

$\frac{7}{12}$	$\frac{3}{4}$	$\frac{5}{6}$	$\frac{3}{4}$	$\frac{3}{8}$	$\frac{1}{4}$

$\frac{6}{10}$	$\frac{4}{5}$	$\frac{1}{2}$	$\frac{5}{12}$	$\frac{3}{7}$	$\frac{4}{10}$

$\frac{4}{5}$	$\frac{3}{4}$	$\frac{5}{12}$	$\frac{3}{7}$	$\frac{9}{10}$	$\frac{11}{12}$

$\frac{3}{10}$	$\frac{35}{100}$	$\frac{7}{8}$	$\frac{9}{10}$	$\frac{5}{7}$	$\frac{4}{5}$

$\frac{80}{10}$	$\frac{3}{4}$	$1\frac{1}{2}$	$\frac{10}{8}$	$\frac{4}{6}$	$\frac{8}{9}$

$\frac{14}{5}$	$2\frac{1}{4}$	$\frac{10}{3}$	$3\frac{1}{4}$	$1\frac{1}{3}$	$\frac{5}{4}$

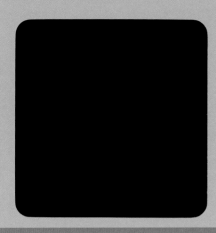

2 Circle the smaller number in each pair.

$\frac{1}{2}$ $\frac{2}{5}$	$\frac{4}{5}$ $\frac{6}{10}$	$\frac{6}{10}$ $\frac{1}{5}$
$\frac{3}{4}$ $\frac{5}{8}$	$\frac{1}{6}$ $\frac{3}{12}$	$\frac{3}{6}$ $\frac{7}{12}$
$\frac{5}{8}$ $\frac{1}{2}$	$\frac{3}{10}$ $\frac{2}{5}$	$1\frac{1}{3}$ $\frac{6}{5}$
$\frac{5}{12}$ $\frac{3}{6}$	$1\frac{4}{10}$ $\frac{9}{5}$	$\frac{12}{4}$ $\frac{30}{8}$
$\frac{80}{10}$ $\frac{75}{100}$	$3\frac{6}{7}$ $3\frac{3}{5}$	$1\frac{9}{10}$ $\frac{18}{12}$
$\frac{31}{4}$ $\frac{44}{8}$	$\frac{9}{10}$ $\frac{11}{12}$	$3\frac{1}{4}$ $\frac{18}{8}$
$\frac{45}{10}$ $4\frac{2}{5}$	$\frac{28}{3}$ $\frac{37}{4}$	$\frac{6}{9}$ $\frac{7}{6}$

More adding and subtracting

You may find it easier to convert mixed numbers to improper fractions before you try and find answers to these sums.

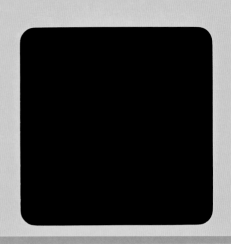

(1) Do the addition.

$\frac{1}{4} + \frac{1}{3} =$ ⬜

$\frac{3}{4} + \frac{1}{5} =$ ⬜

$\frac{2}{3} + \frac{1}{2} =$ ⬜

$\frac{1}{4} + \frac{1}{2} =$ ⬜

$2\frac{1}{2} + 1\frac{1}{4} =$ ⬜

$3\frac{2}{5} + 1\frac{1}{3} =$ ⬜

$1\frac{3}{5} + 1\frac{3}{4} =$ ⬜

$4\frac{1}{2} + 2\frac{2}{5} =$ ⬜

$4\frac{3}{8} + 2\frac{1}{4} =$ ⬜

$3\frac{2}{5} + 1\frac{1}{10} =$ ⬜

$3\frac{3}{5} + 2\frac{3}{5} =$ ⬜

$1\frac{5}{8} + 2\frac{3}{4} =$ ⬜

$\frac{1}{4} + \frac{1}{2} + \frac{3}{4} =$ ⬜

$\frac{3}{4} + \frac{1}{2} + \frac{1}{8} =$ ⬜

$\frac{7}{10} + \frac{4}{10} + \frac{3}{5} =$ ⬜

$\frac{1}{6} + \frac{2}{3} + \frac{1}{2} =$ ⬜

$2\frac{1}{2} + \frac{5}{6} + \frac{1}{3} =$ ⬜

$\frac{1}{2} + \frac{1}{10} + \frac{1}{5} =$ ⬜

Time filler:
Dave's grandmother gives him £20 for Christmas. He spends $\frac{1}{2}$ the money on a computer game and $\frac{1}{5}$ on a comic book. He saves the rest. What fraction of his money does he save? Later, Dave spends $\frac{1}{6}$ of his saved money on sweets. How much do the sweets cost?

2 Do the subtraction.

$\frac{3}{5} - \frac{1}{3} =$ ☐

$\frac{2}{3} - \frac{1}{4} =$ ☐

$\frac{3}{4} - \frac{1}{2} =$ ☐

$\frac{3}{4} - \frac{1}{5} =$ ☐

$\frac{3}{8} - \frac{1}{4} =$ ☐

$\frac{2}{3} - \frac{2}{5} =$ ☐

$\frac{9}{10} - \frac{3}{5} =$ ☐

$\frac{7}{8} - \frac{3}{4} =$ ☐

$\frac{5}{6} - \frac{2}{3} =$ ☐

$2\frac{4}{5} - \frac{1}{5} =$ ☐

$3\frac{1}{2} - 1\frac{3}{4} =$ ☐

$4\frac{1}{3} - 2\frac{1}{2} =$ ☐

$2\frac{1}{3} - \frac{4}{5} =$ ☐

$3\frac{1}{4} - 1\frac{5}{8} =$ ☐

$4\frac{7}{10} - 2\frac{4}{5} =$ ☐

$6\frac{1}{2} - 3\frac{3}{10} =$ ☐

$3\frac{5}{6} - 2\frac{1}{2} =$ ☐

$4\frac{7}{10} - 2\frac{1}{2} =$ ☐

Fractions and decimals

Do you know what numbers written after a decimal point tell you? For example, have you discovered yet that 0.3 is the same as $\frac{3}{10}$, 0.03 is the same as $\frac{3}{100}$, 0.003 is the same as $\frac{3}{1000}$ and so on?

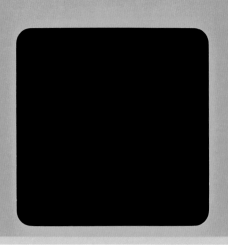

1 Write each decimal as a fraction.

0.1 ▭/▭   0.3 ▭/▭   0.8 ▭/▭   0.6 ▭/▭

0.5 ▭/▭   0.7 ▭/▭   0.4 ▭/▭   0.125 ▭/▭

2 Convert each fraction to its decimal equivalent.

$\frac{1}{2}$ ▭ $\frac{1}{4}$ ▭ $\frac{3}{4}$ ▭

$\frac{2}{5}$ ▭ $\frac{1}{10}$ ▭ $\frac{3}{5}$ ▭

$\frac{4}{5}$ ▭ $\frac{9}{10}$ ▭ $\frac{7}{10}$ ▭

$\frac{1}{5}$ ▭ $\frac{2}{10}$ ▭ $\frac{3}{10}$ ▭

$\frac{1}{8}$ ▭ $\frac{3}{8}$ ▭ $\frac{7}{8}$ ▭

$\frac{5}{8}$ ▭ $\frac{5}{4}$ ▭ $\frac{3}{2}$ ▭

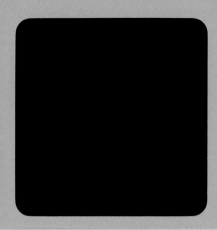

3 Round each number to two decimal places.

1.328　　　2.413　　　0.745　　　1.671

4 Round each number to three decimal places.

0.3787　　　2.4561　　　4.2054

1.8888　　　0.2765　　　0.7632

5 Convert each fraction to its decimal equivalent and give the answer to three decimal places. Use a calculator to help you with the harder sums.

$\frac{1}{8}$ 　　$\frac{3}{8}$ 　　$\frac{1}{12}$

$\frac{7}{8}$ 　　$\frac{5}{8}$ 　　$\frac{1}{3}$

$\frac{2}{3}$ 　　$\frac{4}{7}$ 　　$\frac{7}{12}$

$\frac{9}{16}$ 　　$\frac{4}{12}$ 　　$\frac{8}{15}$

Fractions and percentages 1

If you remember that 1% is the same as the fraction $\frac{1}{100}$, you will have little difficulty writing percentages as fractions and vice versa.

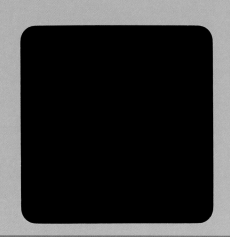

(1) Write each percentage as a fraction in its simplest form.

50% ⬚/⬚   20% ⬚/⬚   70% ⬚/⬚   10% ⬚/⬚

25% ⬚/⬚   75% ⬚/⬚   5% ⬚/⬚   85% ⬚/⬚

80% ⬚/⬚   35% ⬚/⬚   48% ⬚/⬚   18% ⬚/⬚

(2) Write each fraction as a percentage.

$\frac{8}{50}$ ⬚ $\frac{34}{50}$ ⬚ $\frac{42}{50}$ ⬚ $\frac{19}{100}$ ⬚

$\frac{1}{4}$ ⬚ $\frac{65}{100}$ ⬚ $\frac{28}{50}$ ⬚ $\frac{56}{100}$ ⬚

$\frac{3}{4}$ ⬚ $\frac{41}{100}$ ⬚ $\frac{20}{50}$ ⬚ $\frac{45}{50}$ ⬚

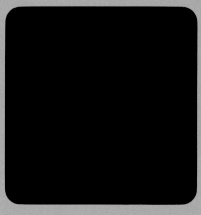

Time filler:
Sean helps his uncle pick apples on the family farm. 10% of the fruit picked is either bruised or overripe and has to be thrown away. Another 15% is given away to friends. What fraction of the apples picked is left to be sold at the market?

3 What is 25% of each amount?

40p ⬚ 60cm ⬚ £4 ⬚ 52g ⬚

4 What is 40% of each amount?

£2 ⬚ 80cm ⬚ £5 ⬚ 10m ⬚

5 Mary bakes a pie for tea. She eats a quarter ($\frac{1}{4}$), serves three-tenths ($\frac{3}{10}$) to her husband and divides the rest equally between her 3 children. What percentage of the pie does each child get?

⬚

6 Circle the fractions that are the same as 60%.

$\frac{3}{5}$ $\frac{18}{20}$ $\frac{30}{50}$ $\frac{90}{150}$ $\frac{60}{90}$ $\frac{40}{70}$

7 Write four fractions that are the same as 30%.

⬚ ⬚ ⬚ ⬚

Fractions and percentages 2

Here is another set of questions on fractions and percentages. They will test how well you have grasped the link between the two.

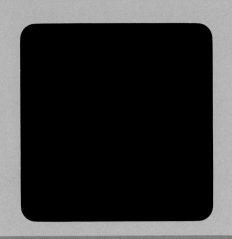

1 Write each fraction as a percentage.

$\frac{7}{10}$ ⬚ $\frac{3}{5}$ ⬚ $\frac{3}{4}$ ⬚ $\frac{9}{10}$ ⬚

2 Increase each amount by $\frac{7}{10}$.

600 km ⬚   12 l ⬚   18 m ⬚   £4 ⬚

3 How much is 30% of each amount?

£2.50 ⬚   7 km ⬚   50 km ⬚   80 p ⬚

4 How much is 90% of each amount?

7 mm ⬚   14 m ⬚   £6 ⬚   80 p ⬚

5 Increase each amount by 25%.

1 800 km ⬚   13 m ⬚   26 mm ⬚   £18 ⬚

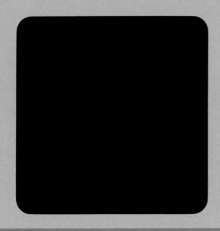

Time filler:
There are 20 children in Mr Brown's maths class. 55% of the children have brown eyes. 35% of them have blue eyes. The rest have green eyes. What fraction of the class has brown eyes, what fraction has blue eyes and what fraction has green eyes?

6 Reduce each amount by 20%.

7 000 km ⬚   £7.50 ⬚   6.5 m ⬚   2.8 cm ⬚

7 Circle the fractions that are equivalent to 12.5%.

$\dfrac{1}{8}$ $\dfrac{3}{16}$ $\dfrac{5}{12}$ $\dfrac{3}{24}$ $\dfrac{2}{4}$

8 Circle the fractions that are larger than 60%.

$\dfrac{2}{5}$ $\dfrac{4}{5}$ $\dfrac{7}{10}$ $\dfrac{3}{4}$ $\dfrac{3}{10}$

9 A TV costs £350 but is reduced by 15% in a sale. How much will it cost in the sale?

10 Petrol costs 130 p per litre. How much will a litre of petrol cost if the price is increased by 10%?

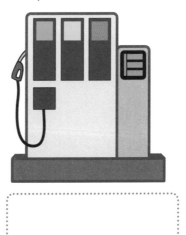

Beat the clock 3

Now test your improved fraction skills.
Work quickly, but remember it is important to
check all the answers. How many sums can you
do in 10 minutes?

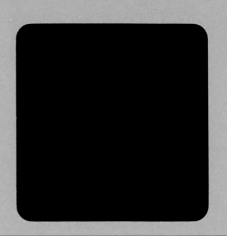

Write each percentage as a fraction in its simplest form.

(1) 25%

(2) 60%

(3) 75%

(4) 10%

(5) 35%

(6) 85%

(7) 50%

(8) 90%

(9) 65%

(10) 30%

(11) 70%

(12) 20%

(13) 40%

(14) 1%

(15) 5%

Write the answer as quickly as you can.

(16) $\frac{1}{2} + \frac{1}{4} =$

(17) $\frac{7}{9} - \frac{6}{9} =$

(18) $\frac{4}{5} \times \frac{1}{2} =$

(19) $\frac{1}{3} + \frac{1}{3} =$

(20) $\frac{7}{8} - \frac{2}{8} =$

(21) $\frac{1}{3} \times \frac{2}{3} =$

(22) $1 - \frac{2}{3} =$

(23) $1 - \frac{3}{5} =$

(24) $\frac{3}{7} \times \frac{2}{5} =$

(25) $\frac{5}{12} + \frac{6}{12} =$

(26) $2 - \frac{3}{2} =$

(27) $2\frac{1}{2} \times 3 =$

(28) $\frac{3}{10} + \frac{6}{10} =$

(29) $3 - 2\frac{1}{3} =$

(30) $4\frac{1}{4} \times 4 =$

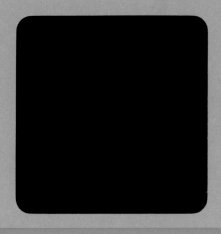

Time filler:
Make a list of what you did today, mentioning the time each activity took, from getting up, washing and dressing up, to going to bed. Work out what percentage of your day you spent on each activity. Convert these percentages to fractions in their simplest form.

Convert each fraction to its decimal equivalent.

(31) $\frac{1}{2}$

(32) $\frac{1}{4}$

(33) $\frac{3}{4}$

(34) $\frac{2}{5}$

(35) $\frac{7}{10}$

(36) $\frac{3}{5}$

(37) $\frac{3}{10}$

(38) $\frac{4}{5}$

(39) $\frac{1}{10}$

(40) $\frac{1}{5}$

(41) $\frac{5}{10}$

(42) $\frac{6}{10}$

Simplify each fraction as far as possible.

(43) $\frac{8}{16}$

(44) $\frac{20}{50}$

(45) $\frac{80}{100}$

(46) $\frac{17}{19}$

(47) $\frac{24}{36}$

(48) $\frac{13}{39}$

(49) $\frac{48}{60}$

(50) $\frac{24}{40}$

(51) $\frac{18}{54}$

(52) $\frac{80}{200}$

(53) $\frac{16}{64}$

(54) $\frac{80}{120}$

(55) $\frac{7}{21}$

(56) $\frac{9}{20}$

(57) $\frac{45}{70}$

(58) $\frac{250}{1000}$

(59) $\frac{60}{600}$

(60) $\frac{21}{63}$

Answers:

04–05 Counting in tenths
06–07 Fractions of numbers, objects and groups

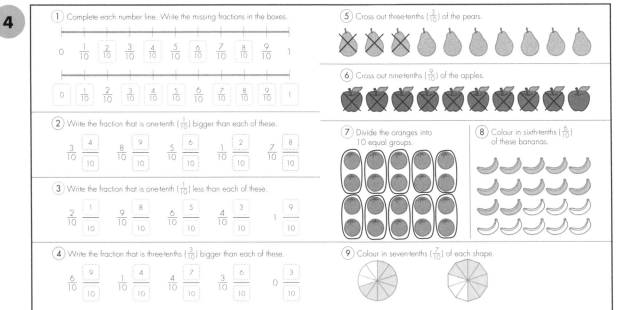

4

1. Complete each number line. Write the missing fractions in the boxes.

$0 \quad \frac{1}{10} \quad \frac{2}{10} \quad \frac{3}{10} \quad \frac{4}{10} \quad \frac{5}{10} \quad \frac{6}{10} \quad \frac{7}{10} \quad \frac{8}{10} \quad \frac{9}{10} \quad 1$

$0 \quad \frac{1}{10} \quad \frac{2}{10} \quad \frac{3}{10} \quad \frac{4}{10} \quad \frac{5}{10} \quad \frac{6}{10} \quad \frac{7}{10} \quad \frac{8}{10} \quad \frac{9}{10} \quad 1$

2. Write the fraction that is one-tenth $\left(\frac{1}{10}\right)$ bigger than each of these.

$\frac{3}{10} \quad \frac{4}{10} \qquad \frac{8}{10} \quad \frac{9}{10} \qquad \frac{5}{10} \quad \frac{6}{10} \qquad \frac{1}{10} \quad \frac{2}{10} \qquad \frac{7}{10} \quad \frac{8}{10}$

3. Write the fraction that is one-tenth $\left(\frac{1}{10}\right)$ less than each of these.

$\frac{2}{10} \quad \frac{1}{10} \qquad \frac{9}{10} \quad \frac{8}{10} \qquad \frac{6}{10} \quad \frac{5}{10} \qquad \frac{4}{10} \quad \frac{3}{10} \qquad 1 \quad \frac{9}{10}$

4. Write the fraction that is three-tenths $\left(\frac{3}{10}\right)$ bigger than each of these.

$\frac{6}{10} \quad \frac{9}{10} \qquad \frac{1}{10} \quad \frac{4}{10} \qquad \frac{4}{10} \quad \frac{7}{10} \qquad \frac{3}{10} \quad \frac{6}{10} \qquad 0 \quad \frac{3}{10}$

5

5. Cross out three-tenths $\left(\frac{3}{10}\right)$ of the pears.

6. Cross out nine-tenths $\left(\frac{9}{10}\right)$ of the apples.

7. Divide the oranges into 10 equal groups.

8. Colour in sixth-tenths $\left(\frac{6}{10}\right)$ of these bananas.

9. Colour in seven-tenths $\left(\frac{7}{10}\right)$ of each shape.

Your child should be very familiar with counting in tens up to any number. At this stage however, they must learn to go "into reverse" and think about tenths, and begin to understand some simple relationships. For example: five-tenths is equivalent to one-half, and one-tenth is the same as 10 p in relation to the pound.

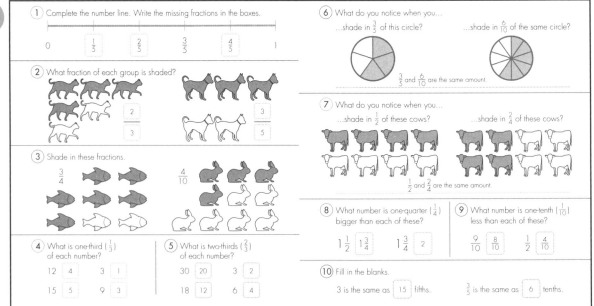

6

1. Complete the number line. Write the missing fractions in the boxes.

$0 \quad \frac{1}{5} \quad \frac{2}{5} \quad \frac{3}{5} \quad \frac{4}{5} \quad 1$

2. What fraction of each group is shaded?

$\frac{2}{3} \qquad \frac{3}{5}$

3. Shade in these fractions.

$\frac{3}{4} \qquad \frac{4}{10}$

4. What is one-third $\left(\frac{1}{3}\right)$ of each number?

| 12 | 4 | 3 | 1 |
| 15 | 5 | 9 | 3 |

5. What is two-thirds $\left(\frac{2}{3}\right)$ of each number?

| 30 | 20 | 3 | 2 |
| 18 | 12 | 6 | 4 |

7

6. What do you notice when you…
…shade in $\frac{3}{5}$ of this circle? …shade in $\frac{6}{10}$ of the same circle?

$\frac{3}{5}$ and $\frac{6}{10}$ are the same amount.

7. What do you notice when you…
…shade in $\frac{1}{2}$ of these cows? …shade in $\frac{2}{4}$ of these cows?

$\frac{1}{2}$ and $\frac{2}{4}$ are the same amount.

8. What number is one-quarter $\left(\frac{1}{4}\right)$ bigger than each of these?

$1\frac{1}{2} \quad 1\frac{3}{4} \qquad 1\frac{3}{4} \quad 2$

9. What number is one-tenth $\left(\frac{1}{10}\right)$ less than each of these?

$\frac{9}{10} \quad \frac{8}{10} \qquad \frac{1}{2} \quad \frac{4}{10}$

10. Fill in the blanks.

3 is the same as 15 fifths. $\frac{3}{5}$ is the same as 6 tenths.

Your child usually begins to understand fractions through shading or colouring parts of shapes like squares and circles. It is important that he or she quickly translates the understanding into more practical situations, such as finding fractions of actual objects and amounts of money.

Answers:

08–09 Fractions and division 1
10–11 Fractions and division 2

8

① What is half ($\frac{1}{2}$) of each amount?

| 8g | 4g | 4cm | 2cm | 10m | 5m | 2p | 1p |

| 10p | 5p | 20p | 10p | 6p | 3p | 12p | 6p |

② Divide each number by 2.

| 4 | 2 | 2 | 1 | 8 | 4 | 10 | 5 |

| 20 | 10 | 12 | 6 | 14 | 7 | 6 | 3 |

③ What is one-third ($\frac{1}{3}$) of each number?

| 6 | 2 | 12 | 4 | 3 | 1 | 15 | 5 |

| 24 | 8 | 39 | 13 | 18 | 6 | 36 | 12 |

9

④ Divide each amount by 3.

| 12p | 4p | 6g | 2g | 15cm | 5cm | 3p | 1p |

⑤ What is two-thirds ($\frac{2}{3}$) of each amount?

| 9g | 6g | 18cm | 12cm | 30m | 20m | 3p | 2p |

| 6p | 4p | 12cm | 8cm | 18g | 12g | 15p | 10p |

⑥ What is one-quarter ($\frac{1}{4}$) of each amount?

| 4p | 1p | 20g | 5g | 16cm | 4cm | 8p | 2p |

⑦ Divide each number by 4.

| 16 | 4 | 4 | 1 | 12 | 3 | 20 | 5 |

Your child needs to understand that finding a fraction, such as a quarter, is equivalent to dividing by four. Many children never grasp this correspondence and that can hinder further progress. Likewise, with more complicated fractions, such as three-quarters, your child must realise that this is equivalent to dividing by four and then multiplying by three.

10

① What is three-quarters ($\frac{3}{4}$) of each amount?

| 8g | 6g | 4cm | 3cm | 12m | 9m | 20p | 15p |

| 16p | 12p | 24g | 18g | 40cm | 30cm | 4p | 3p |

② What is one-tenth ($\frac{1}{10}$) of each amount?

| 50p | 5p | 10cm | 1cm | 30g | 3g | 80cm | 8cm |

③ Divide each number by 10.

| 20 | 2 | 50 | 5 | 10 | 1 | 30 | 3 |

④ What is two-quarters ($\frac{2}{4}$) of each number?

| 18 | 9 | 16 | 8 | 40 | 20 | 6 | 3 |

11

⑤ What is one-fifth ($\frac{1}{5}$) of each amount?

| 25p | 5p | 5cm | 1cm | 50g | 10g | 10cm | 2cm |

⑥ Divide each number by 5.

| 15 | 3 | 25 | 5 | 5 | 1 | 20 | 4 |

⑦ Jane buys a bar of chocolate weighing 100g. She uses two-fifths ($\frac{2}{5}$) of it to make a cake and eats the rest. How much chocolate goes into the cake?

| 40g |

⑧ What is five-tenths ($\frac{5}{10}$) of each number?

| 10 | 5 | 30 | 15 | 60 | 30 | 100 | 50 |

Your child should continue to practise these types of problem; the more the better. Although your child can often find his or her own "short cuts" to solutions, he or she should be taught to first divide by the denominator and then multiply by the numerator.

Answers:

12–13 Fractions and division 3
14–15 Equivalent fractions 1

12

1. Write each fraction in words.
$\frac{1}{2}$ One-half $\frac{1}{4}$ One-quarter
$\frac{1}{10}$ One-tenth $\frac{1}{3}$ One-third

2. Write each fraction in numbers.
Two-fifths $\frac{2}{5}$ Three-quarters $\frac{3}{4}$ Two-tenths $\frac{2}{10}$

3. What is two-thirds $(\frac{2}{3})$ of each amount?
21 p 14p   33 cm 22cm   60 g 40g   27 p 18p

4. What is four-fifths $(\frac{4}{5})$ of each number?
25 20   45 36   50 40   5 4

5. What is seven-tenths $(\frac{7}{10})$ of each amount?
30g 21g   60cm 42cm   120m 84m   10p 7p

13

6. What fraction of 30 is each number?
15 $\frac{1}{2}$ 3 $\frac{1}{10}$ 10 $\frac{1}{3}$ 6 $\frac{1}{5}$

7. What fraction of 24 is each number?
8 $\frac{1}{3}$ 6 $\frac{1}{4}$ 12 $\frac{1}{2}$ 16 $\frac{2}{3}$

8. What fraction of 10 is each number?
5 $\frac{1}{2}$ 1 $\frac{1}{10}$ 6 $\frac{3}{5}$ 9 $\frac{9}{10}$

9. What fraction of 50 is each number?
10 $\frac{1}{5}$ 5 $\frac{1}{10}$ 25 $\frac{1}{2}$ 30 $\frac{3}{5}$

10. What fraction of 60 is each number?
6 $\frac{1}{10}$ 12 $\frac{1}{5}$ 30 $\frac{1}{2}$ 20 $\frac{1}{3}$

Continuing with this practice of fractions and their usefulness, your child needs to realise the importance of a good knowledge of times tables. Your child should not only be able to recall times tables, but he or she must be able to do it accurately and quickly. Sometimes, the "quickly" part may be neglected.

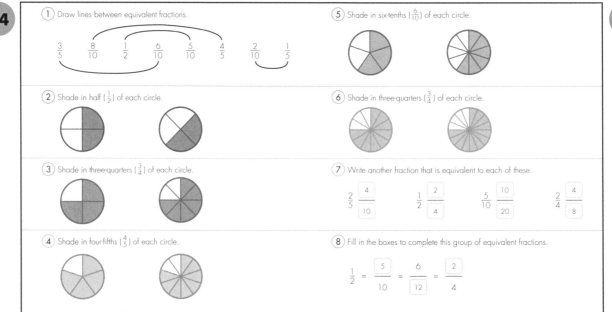

14–15

1. Draw lines between equivalent fractions.
$\frac{3}{5}$ $\frac{8}{10}$ $\frac{1}{2}$ $\frac{6}{10}$ $\frac{5}{10}$ $\frac{4}{5}$ $\frac{2}{10}$ $\frac{1}{5}$

2. Shade in half $(\frac{1}{2})$ of each circle.
3. Shade in three-quarters $(\frac{3}{4})$ of each circle.
4. Shade in four-fifths $(\frac{4}{5})$ of each circle.
5. Shade in six-tenths $(\frac{6}{10})$ of each circle.
6. Shade in three-quarters $(\frac{3}{4})$ of each circle.

7. Write another fraction that is equivalent to each of these.
$\frac{2}{5}$ $\frac{4}{10}$ $\frac{1}{2}$ $\frac{2}{4}$ $\frac{5}{10}$ $\frac{10}{20}$ $\frac{2}{4}$ $\frac{4}{8}$

8. Fill in the boxes to complete this group of equivalent fractions.
$\frac{1}{2} = \frac{5}{10} = \frac{6}{12} = \frac{2}{4}$

The ability to simplify fractions is very important and relies on children "seeing" connections between the numerator and the denominator. For example: the act of simplifying $\frac{7}{21}$ relies on your child having a firm knowledge of the seven times tables. It is useful to understand that if both the numerator and the denominator are even, they can both be divided by two.

Answers:

16–17 Adding fractions 1
18–19 Subtracting fractions 1
20–21 Beat the clock 1, see p.80

---

16 **17**

① Add the fractions and simplify the answers.

$\frac{1}{2}+\frac{1}{2}=\frac{2}{2}=1$ $\frac{2}{3}+\frac{1}{3}=\frac{3}{3}=1$ $\frac{3}{10}+\frac{3}{10}=\frac{6}{10}=\frac{3}{5}$

$\frac{1}{5}+\frac{4}{5}=\frac{5}{5}=1$ $\frac{3}{6}+\frac{1}{6}=\frac{4}{6}=\frac{2}{3}$ $\frac{6}{10}+\frac{4}{10}=\frac{10}{10}=1$

$\frac{6}{7}+\frac{1}{7}=\frac{7}{7}=1$ $\frac{3}{5}+\frac{2}{5}=\frac{5}{5}=1$ $\frac{5}{10}+\frac{3}{10}=\frac{8}{10}=\frac{4}{5}$

$\frac{5}{6}+\frac{1}{6}=\frac{6}{6}=1$ $\frac{2}{7}+\frac{5}{7}=\frac{7}{7}=1$ $\frac{8}{10}+\frac{2}{10}=\frac{10}{10}=1$

② Add these fractions. Simplify any answer you can.

$\frac{1}{5}+\frac{1}{5}=\boxed{\frac{2}{5}}$ $\frac{1}{4}+\frac{1}{4}=\boxed{\frac{1}{2}}$ $\frac{5}{7}+\frac{1}{7}=\boxed{\frac{6}{7}}$

$\frac{4}{6}+\frac{1}{6}=\boxed{\frac{5}{6}}$ $\frac{1}{5}+\frac{2}{5}=\boxed{\frac{3}{5}}$ $\frac{6}{10}+\frac{2}{10}=\boxed{\frac{4}{5}}$

$\frac{3}{6}+\frac{1}{6}=\boxed{\frac{2}{3}}$ $\frac{3}{5}+\frac{1}{5}=\boxed{\frac{4}{5}}$ $\frac{4}{10}+\frac{5}{10}=\boxed{\frac{9}{10}}$

$\frac{2}{7}+\frac{3}{7}=\boxed{\frac{5}{7}}$ $\frac{1}{3}+\frac{1}{3}=\boxed{\frac{2}{3}}$ $\frac{3}{10}+\frac{6}{10}=\boxed{\frac{9}{10}}$

$\frac{4}{6}+\frac{1}{6}=\boxed{\frac{5}{6}}$ $\frac{1}{4}+\frac{1}{4}+\frac{1}{4}=\boxed{\frac{3}{4}}$ $\frac{1}{5}+\frac{1}{5}+\frac{1}{5}=\boxed{\frac{3}{5}}$

③ Darius adds one-fifth ($\frac{1}{5}$) of 10 to two-fifths ($\frac{2}{5}$) of 20.

What answer does he arrive at? $\boxed{10}$

④ Emmie adds a quarter ($\frac{1}{4}$) of 12 to three-quarters ($\frac{3}{4}$) of 16.

What answer does she arrive at? $\boxed{15}$

⑤ Clara adds six-tenths ($\frac{6}{10}$) of 30 p to three-tenths ($\frac{3}{10}$) of 20 p.

How much does Clara now have? $\boxed{24\,\text{p}}$

⑥ David adds three-quarters ($\frac{3}{4}$) of 40 p to one-quarter ($\frac{1}{4}$) of 16 p.

How much does David now have? $\boxed{34\,\text{p}}$

⑦ Answer these questions.

Add $\frac{3}{5}$ of 25 to $\frac{2}{5}$ of 25. $\boxed{25}$

How much is $\frac{7}{10}$ of 20 added to $\frac{1}{10}$ of 20? $\boxed{16}$

How much is $\frac{6}{10}$ of £10 added to $\frac{2}{10}$ of £10? $\boxed{£8}$

Your child will usually find adding fractions with a common denominator very straightforward. It is very important, however, that he or she understands what is happening in the process. He or she must also learn to quickly recognise how an answer such as $\frac{5}{10}$ may be simplified.

---

18 **19**

① Subtract these fractions. Simplify any answer you can.

$\frac{1}{2}-\frac{1}{2}=\boxed{0}$ $\frac{2}{3}-\frac{1}{3}=\boxed{\frac{1}{3}}$ $\frac{8}{3}-\frac{6}{3}=\boxed{\frac{2}{3}}$

$\frac{6}{4}-\frac{3}{4}=\boxed{\frac{3}{4}}$ $\frac{3}{4}-\frac{2}{4}=\boxed{\frac{1}{4}}$ $\frac{8}{4}-\frac{3}{4}=\boxed{\frac{5}{4}}$

$\frac{4}{5}-\frac{3}{5}=\boxed{\frac{1}{5}}$ $\frac{3}{5}-\frac{2}{5}=\boxed{\frac{1}{5}}$ $\frac{4}{5}-\frac{1}{5}=\boxed{\frac{3}{5}}$

$\frac{4}{6}-\frac{3}{6}=\boxed{\frac{1}{6}}$ $\frac{8}{6}-\frac{2}{6}=\boxed{1}$ $\frac{9}{6}-\frac{1}{6}=\boxed{\frac{4}{3}}$

$\frac{6}{7}-\frac{4}{7}=\boxed{\frac{2}{7}}$ $\frac{2}{7}-\frac{1}{7}=\boxed{\frac{1}{7}}$ $\frac{5}{7}-\frac{3}{7}=\boxed{\frac{2}{7}}$

$\frac{4}{8}-\frac{4}{8}=\boxed{0}$ $\frac{4}{8}-\frac{3}{8}=\boxed{\frac{1}{8}}$ $\frac{7}{8}-\frac{5}{8}=\boxed{\frac{1}{4}}$

$\frac{4}{9}-\frac{2}{9}=\boxed{\frac{2}{9}}$ $\frac{5}{9}-\frac{1}{9}=\boxed{\frac{4}{9}}$ $\frac{6}{9}-\frac{6}{9}=\boxed{0}$

$\frac{8}{10}-\frac{3}{10}=\boxed{\frac{1}{2}}$ $\frac{6}{10}-\frac{5}{10}=\boxed{\frac{1}{10}}$ $\frac{9}{10}-\frac{3}{10}=\boxed{\frac{3}{5}}$

$\frac{7}{10}-\frac{4}{10}=\boxed{\frac{3}{10}}$ $\frac{9}{10}-\frac{5}{10}=\boxed{\frac{2}{5}}$ $\frac{5}{10}-\frac{1}{10}=\boxed{\frac{2}{5}}$

② Write the answer in the box.

$1-\frac{1}{2}=\boxed{\frac{1}{2}}$ $1-\frac{1}{3}=\boxed{\frac{2}{3}}$ $1-\frac{1}{4}=\boxed{\frac{3}{4}}$

$1-\frac{6}{7}=\boxed{\frac{1}{7}}$ $1-\frac{6}{8}=\boxed{\frac{2}{8}}$ $1-\frac{7}{10}=\boxed{\frac{3}{10}}$

③ Katie eats $\frac{2}{5}$ of her birthday cake and her sister eats $\frac{1}{5}$ of it. How much of the cake is left?

$\boxed{\dfrac{2}{5}}$

④ $\frac{3}{8}$ of a pizza is eaten by Barbara and $\frac{2}{8}$ by Ann. Harry eats the rest. What fraction of pizza does Harry eat?

$\boxed{\dfrac{3}{8}}$

⑤ What is the difference between three-fifths ($\frac{3}{5}$) of 20 p and two-fifths ($\frac{2}{5}$) of 20 p?

$\boxed{4\,\text{p}}$

⑥ Write the missing fractions.

$\frac{2}{7}+\boxed{\frac{4}{7}}+\frac{1}{7}=1$ $\frac{4}{10}+\boxed{\frac{4}{10}}+\frac{2}{10}=1$

Subtracting fractions with the same denominator is straightforward, but your child should know how to convert whole numbers and mixed numbers into fractions with the appropriate denominator. For example: $1-\frac{2}{5}$ needs your child to convert the 1 into $\frac{5}{5}$ first and then do the subtraction.

70

Answers:

22–23 Comparing and ordering fractions
24–25 Counting in hundreths

22

① Circle the smaller fraction in each pair.

($\frac{1}{4}$) $\frac{3}{4}$ ($\frac{1}{3}$) $\frac{2}{3}$ $\frac{4}{5}$ ($\frac{2}{5}$) ($\frac{1}{10}$) $\frac{7}{10}$

$\frac{6}{5}$ ($\frac{1}{5}$) ($\frac{4}{6}$) $\frac{5}{6}$ $\frac{5}{6}$ ($\frac{1}{6}$) $\frac{8}{10}$ ($\frac{3}{10}$)

($\frac{2}{7}$) $\frac{4}{7}$ $\frac{7}{8}$ ($\frac{4}{8}$) $\frac{3}{5}$ ($\frac{1}{5}$) · $\frac{8}{9}$ ($\frac{7}{9}$)

($\frac{3}{7}$) $\frac{5}{7}$ ($\frac{2}{8}$) $\frac{4}{8}$ $\frac{5}{8}$ ($\frac{3}{8}$) ($\frac{7}{10}$) $\frac{9}{10}$

② Circle the larger fraction in each pair.

($\frac{3}{5}$) $\frac{1}{5}$ ($\frac{4}{5}$) $\frac{3}{5}$ ($\frac{5}{8}$) $\frac{4}{8}$ ($\frac{2}{10}$) $\frac{1}{10}$

($\frac{3}{7}$) $\frac{1}{7}$ $\frac{2}{9}$ ($\frac{4}{9}$) ($\frac{3}{4}$) $\frac{2}{4}$ $\frac{3}{10}$ ($\frac{4}{10}$)

($\frac{5}{6}$) $\frac{2}{6}$ $\frac{5}{7}$ ($\frac{6}{7}$) ($\frac{5}{6}$) $\frac{2}{6}$ ($\frac{5}{8}$) $\frac{3}{8}$

($\frac{2}{3}$) $\frac{1}{3}$ $\frac{3}{5}$ ($\frac{4}{5}$) $\frac{3}{9}$ ($\frac{5}{9}$) $\frac{1}{4}$ ($\frac{2}{4}$)

23

③ Write the fractions in order, starting with the smallest.

$\frac{4}{5}$ $\frac{1}{5}$ $\frac{5}{5}$ → [$\frac{1}{5}$] [$\frac{4}{5}$] [$\frac{5}{5}$] $\frac{7}{10}$ $\frac{3}{10}$ $\frac{5}{10}$ → [$\frac{3}{10}$] [$\frac{5}{10}$] [$\frac{7}{10}$]

$\frac{7}{8}$ $\frac{4}{8}$ $\frac{2}{8}$ → [$\frac{2}{8}$] [$\frac{4}{8}$] [$\frac{7}{8}$] $\frac{9}{10}$ $\frac{6}{10}$ $\frac{8}{10}$ → [$\frac{6}{10}$] [$\frac{8}{10}$] [$\frac{9}{10}$]

④ Write the fractions in order, starting with the largest.

$\frac{8}{9}$ $\frac{3}{9}$ $\frac{5}{9}$ $\frac{7}{9}$ → [$\frac{8}{9}$] [$\frac{7}{9}$] [$\frac{5}{9}$] [$\frac{3}{9}$] $\frac{8}{8}$ $\frac{4}{8}$ $\frac{2}{8}$ $\frac{5}{8}$ → [$\frac{8}{8}$] [$\frac{5}{8}$] [$\frac{4}{8}$] [$\frac{2}{8}$]

$\frac{2}{7}$ $\frac{4}{7}$ $\frac{1}{7}$ $\frac{6}{7}$ → [$\frac{6}{7}$] [$\frac{4}{7}$] [$\frac{2}{7}$] [$\frac{1}{7}$] $\frac{4}{10}$ $\frac{7}{10}$ $\frac{5}{10}$ $\frac{8}{10}$ → [$\frac{8}{10}$] [$\frac{7}{10}$] [$\frac{5}{10}$] [$\frac{4}{10}$]

⑤ Write the fractions in order, starting with the smallest.

$\frac{6}{10}$ $\frac{2}{10}$ $\frac{5}{10}$ $\frac{8}{10}$ $\frac{7}{10}$ $\frac{3}{10}$ → [$\frac{2}{10}$] [$\frac{3}{10}$] [$\frac{5}{10}$] [$\frac{6}{10}$] [$\frac{7}{10}$] [$\frac{8}{10}$]

A fraction "number line" can help your child recognise their order. If your child is struggling, simply draw a line and put 0 at the left end and 1 at the right. Now work with your child to roughly place the appropriate fractions on the line. For example: the same line, with tenths marked on, can be used for many questions.

24

① Write each amount as a hundredth of a pound (£).
Note: £1 = 100 pence. 1p = $\frac{1}{100}$ × £1

5p $\frac{5}{100}$ 13p $\frac{13}{100}$ 8p $\frac{8}{100}$ 15p $\frac{15}{100}$

21p $\frac{21}{100}$ 18p $\frac{18}{100}$ 26p $\frac{26}{100}$ 2p $\frac{2}{100}$

40p $\frac{40}{100}$ 58p $\frac{58}{100}$ 67p $\frac{67}{100}$ 95p $\frac{95}{100}$

② Write each amount as a hundredth of a metre (m).
Note: 1 metre = 100 centimetres. 1 cm = $\frac{1}{100}$ × 1 m

4cm $\frac{4}{100}$ 27cm $\frac{27}{100}$ 53cm $\frac{53}{100}$ 88cm $\frac{88}{100}$

③ A new TV costs £300. Paul has saved $\frac{40}{100}$ of the amount. How much more must he save?

£180

25

④ Fill in the missing fractions to complete each sequence.

$\frac{10}{100}$ $\frac{20}{100}$ $\frac{30}{100}$ $\frac{40}{100}$ $\frac{50}{100}$ $\frac{60}{100}$ $\frac{70}{100}$ $\frac{80}{100}$ $\frac{90}{100}$

$\frac{100}{100}$ $\frac{90}{100}$ $\frac{80}{100}$ $\frac{70}{100}$ $\frac{60}{100}$ $\frac{50}{100}$ $\frac{40}{100}$ $\frac{30}{100}$ $\frac{20}{100}$ $\frac{10}{100}$

⑤ A class raises £100 for a Christmas party.
They spend $\frac{60}{100}$ on the party.
The rest they give to charity.
How much do they give to charity?

£40

⑥ How much is one-hundredth ($\frac{1}{100}$) of each amount?

£2 [2p] 3.5m [3.5cm] 60m [60cm] 10m [10cm]

9m [9cm] £20 [20p] £100 [£1] 70m [70cm]

£6 [6p] £400 [£4] £19 [19p] £130 [£1.30]

Here, counting in hundredths is particularly associated with pence in a pound (sterling) and centimetres in a metre, because it helps make the problems more realistic.

Answers:

26–27 Harder fractions
28–29 Equivalent fractions 2

26 **27**

(1) Work out five-sixths ($\frac{5}{6}$) of each amount.

18g [15g]   30cm [25cm]   60kg [50kg]   72p [60p]

(2) What is nine-tenths ($\frac{9}{10}$) of each amount?

130kg [117kg]   250g [225g]   80p [72p]   10p [9p]

(3) How many days are there in five-sevenths ($\frac{5}{7}$) of each period of time?

3 weeks [15 days]   12 weeks [60 days]

7 weeks [35 days]   20 weeks [100 days]

(4) What fraction of the larger number is the smaller number?

6 is $\frac{1}{3}$ of 18   5 is $\frac{1}{4}$ of 20   18 is $\frac{1}{2}$ of 36

(5) What fraction of the larger amount is the smaller amount?

3p and £3 $\frac{1}{100}$ 1.5m and 6m $\frac{1}{4}$

(6) Work out these word problems.

Oliver has 100 toy bricks. $\frac{9}{10}$ of the bricks are red. How many bricks are not red?

[10] bricks

Katie buys a dozen apples but $\frac{1}{6}$ are rotten. How many apples are not rotten?

[10] apples

(7) How long is two-thirds ($\frac{2}{3}$) of each lesson? Give your answer in minutes.

The lesson is half-an-hour long.   [20 minutes]

The lesson is 1 hour long.   [40 minutes]

The lesson is $2\frac{1}{2}$ hours long.   [100 minutes]

(8) In each pair, the smaller number is the same fraction of the bigger number. What is the fraction?

32 (28)   64 (56)   40 (35)   80 (32)   150 (60)   200 (80)

$\frac{7}{8}$ $\frac{2}{5}$

It is important for your child to realise that fractions do not just exist in order to torment him or her! He or she should realise that fractions are very useful in everyday life, although decimals are used more often in calculations.

28 **29**

(1) Circle the fractions that are equivalent to one-quarter ($\frac{1}{4}$).

($\frac{2}{8}$) $\frac{5}{20}$ $\frac{6}{30}$ ($\frac{40}{160}$) $\frac{7}{26}$ ($\frac{100}{400}$)

(2) Circle the fractions that are equivalent to two-fifths ($\frac{2}{5}$).

$\frac{4}{8}$ ($\frac{20}{50}$)   ($\frac{22}{55}$)   ($\frac{8}{20}$) $\frac{3}{6}$ ($\frac{400}{1000}$)

(3) Circle the fractions that are equivalent to seven-tenths ($\frac{7}{10}$).

($\frac{14}{20}$)   ($\frac{21}{30}$) $\frac{28}{50}$ ($\frac{70}{100}$) $\frac{42}{70}$ $\frac{8}{11}$

(4) Solve these sums.

What is $\frac{9}{10}$ of £1? [90p]   How long is $\frac{7}{100}$ of 3m? [21cm]

What is $\frac{7}{100}$ of £2? [14p]   How much is $\frac{3}{10}$ of 5kg? [1500g]

(5) Fill in the boxes to complete this group of equivalent fractions.

$\frac{6}{8} = \frac{54}{72} = \frac{60}{80} = \frac{12}{16} = \frac{72}{96}$

(6) A chessboard is square. It is divided into 64 smaller squares.

How many small squares are there on $\frac{7}{8}$ of the board? [56] squares

How many small squares are there on $\frac{3}{4}$ of the board? [48] squares

(7) Simplify each fraction.

$\frac{20}{30}$ [$\frac{2}{3}$] $\frac{12}{18}$ [$\frac{2}{3}$] $\frac{16}{48}$ [$\frac{1}{3}$] $\frac{70}{100}$ [$\frac{7}{10}$]

$\frac{18}{36}$ [$\frac{1}{2}$] $\frac{19}{76}$ [$\frac{1}{4}$] $\frac{72}{96}$ [$\frac{3}{4}$] $\frac{2000}{3000}$ [$\frac{2}{3}$]

(8) Write four more equivalent fractions for each fraction.

$\frac{3}{5} = \frac{6}{10} = \frac{9}{15} = \frac{12}{20} = \frac{15}{25}$ $\frac{5}{12} = \frac{10}{24} = \frac{15}{36} = \frac{20}{48} = \frac{25}{60}$

$\frac{7}{8} = \frac{14}{16} = \frac{21}{24} = \frac{28}{32} = \frac{35}{40}$ $\frac{9}{10} = \frac{18}{20} = \frac{27}{30} = \frac{36}{40} = \frac{45}{50}$

Recognising the equivalence between fractions can help to simplify all sorts of problems and your child should quickly "spot" connections between the numerator and the denominator to speed up the process.

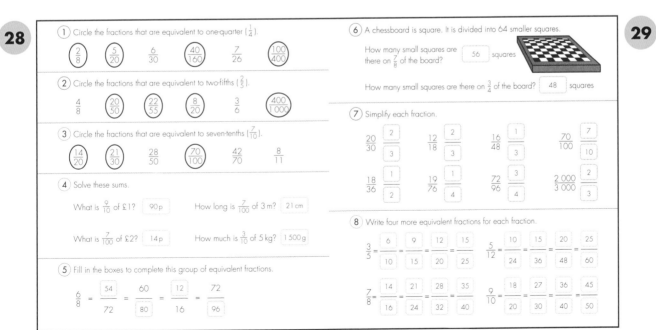

Answers:

30–31 Adding fractions 2
32–33 Subtracting fractions 2

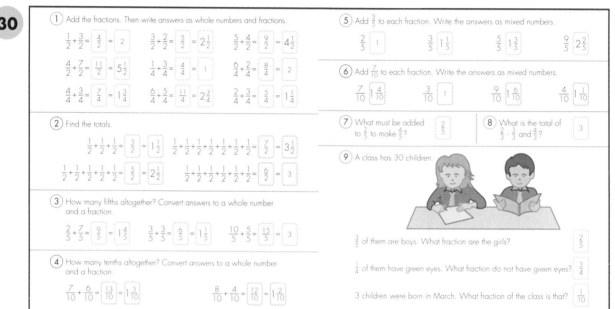

30

(1) Add the fractions. Then write answers as whole numbers and fractions.

$\frac{1}{2}+\frac{3}{2}=\frac{4}{2}=2$ $\frac{3}{2}+\frac{2}{2}=\frac{5}{2}=2\frac{1}{2}$ $\frac{5}{2}+\frac{4}{2}=\frac{9}{2}=4\frac{1}{2}$

$\frac{4}{2}+\frac{7}{2}=\frac{11}{2}=5\frac{1}{2}$ $\frac{1}{4}+\frac{3}{4}=\frac{4}{4}=1$ $\frac{6}{4}+\frac{2}{4}=\frac{8}{4}=2$

$\frac{4}{4}+\frac{3}{4}=\frac{7}{4}=1\frac{3}{4}$ $\frac{6}{4}+\frac{5}{4}=\frac{11}{4}=2\frac{3}{4}$ $\frac{2}{4}+\frac{3}{4}=\frac{5}{4}=1\frac{1}{4}$

(2) Find the totals.

$\frac{1}{2}+\frac{1}{2}+\frac{1}{2}=\frac{3}{2}=1\frac{1}{2}$ $\frac{1}{2}+\frac{1}{2}+\frac{1}{2}+\frac{1}{2}+\frac{1}{2}+\frac{1}{2}+\frac{1}{2}=\frac{7}{2}=3\frac{1}{2}$

$\frac{1}{2}+\frac{1}{2}+\frac{1}{2}+\frac{1}{2}+\frac{1}{2}=\frac{5}{2}=2\frac{1}{2}$ $\frac{1}{2}+\frac{1}{2}+\frac{1}{2}+\frac{1}{2}+\frac{1}{2}+\frac{1}{2}=\frac{6}{2}=3$

(3) How many fifths altogether? Convert answers to a whole number and a fraction.

$\frac{2}{5}+\frac{7}{5}=\frac{9}{5}=1\frac{4}{5}$ $\frac{3}{5}+\frac{3}{5}=\frac{6}{5}=1\frac{1}{5}$ $\frac{10}{5}+\frac{5}{5}=\frac{15}{5}=3$

(4) How many tenths altogether? Convert answers to a whole number and a fraction.

$\frac{7}{10}+\frac{6}{10}=\frac{13}{10}=1\frac{3}{10}$ $\frac{8}{10}+\frac{4}{10}=\frac{12}{10}=1\frac{2}{10}$

31

(5) Add $\frac{3}{5}$ to each fraction. Write the answers as mixed numbers.

$\frac{2}{5}$ $\boxed{1}$ $\frac{3}{5}$ $\boxed{1\frac{1}{5}}$ $\frac{5}{5}$ $\boxed{1\frac{3}{5}}$ $\frac{9}{5}$ $\boxed{2\frac{2}{5}}$

(6) Add $\frac{7}{10}$ to each fraction. Write the answers as mixed numbers.

$\frac{7}{10}$ $\boxed{1\frac{4}{10}}$ $\frac{3}{10}$ $\boxed{1}$ $\frac{9}{10}$ $\boxed{1\frac{6}{10}}$ $\frac{4}{10}$ $\boxed{1\frac{1}{10}}$

(7) What must be added to $\frac{2}{5}$ to make $\frac{4}{5}$? $\boxed{\frac{2}{5}}$

(8) What is the total of $\frac{2}{3}, \frac{3}{3}$ and $\frac{4}{3}$? $\boxed{3}$

(9) A class has 30 children.

$\frac{3}{5}$ of them are boys. What fraction are the girls? $\boxed{\frac{2}{5}}$

$\frac{1}{4}$ of them have green eyes. What fraction do not have green eyes? $\boxed{\frac{3}{4}}$

3 children were born in March. What fraction of the class is that? $\boxed{\frac{1}{10}}$

Most of these fraction additions end up with an answer which is greater than one whole. Hence, your child should begin to recognise these situations and convert the answer into mixed numbers, that is a whole number with a fractional amount. For example: $\frac{3}{2}$ can also be written as $1\frac{1}{2}$.

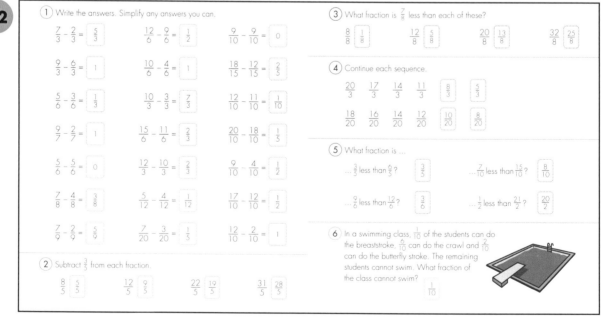

32

(1) Write the answers. Simplify any answers you can.

$\frac{7}{3}-\frac{2}{3}=\boxed{\frac{5}{3}}$ $\frac{12}{6}-\frac{9}{6}=\boxed{\frac{1}{2}}$ $\frac{9}{10}-\frac{9}{10}=\boxed{0}$

$\frac{9}{3}-\frac{6}{3}=\boxed{1}$ $\frac{10}{6}-\frac{4}{6}=\boxed{1}$ $\frac{18}{15}-\frac{12}{15}=\boxed{\frac{2}{5}}$

$\frac{5}{6}-\frac{3}{6}=\boxed{\frac{1}{3}}$ $\frac{10}{3}-\frac{3}{3}=\boxed{\frac{7}{3}}$ $\frac{12}{10}-\frac{11}{10}=\boxed{\frac{1}{10}}$

$\frac{9}{7}-\frac{2}{7}=\boxed{1}$ $\frac{15}{6}-\frac{11}{6}=\boxed{\frac{2}{3}}$ $\frac{20}{10}-\frac{18}{10}=\boxed{\frac{1}{5}}$

$\frac{5}{6}-\frac{5}{6}=\boxed{0}$ $\frac{12}{3}-\frac{10}{3}=\boxed{\frac{2}{3}}$ $\frac{9}{10}-\frac{4}{10}=\boxed{\frac{1}{2}}$

$\frac{7}{8}-\frac{4}{8}=\boxed{\frac{3}{8}}$ $\frac{5}{12}-\frac{4}{12}=\boxed{\frac{1}{12}}$ $\frac{17}{10}-\frac{12}{10}=\boxed{\frac{1}{2}}$

$\frac{7}{9}-\frac{2}{9}=\boxed{\frac{5}{9}}$ $\frac{7}{20}-\frac{3}{20}=\boxed{\frac{1}{5}}$ $\frac{12}{10}-\frac{2}{10}=\boxed{1}$

(2) Subtract $\frac{3}{5}$ from each fraction.

$\frac{8}{5}$ $\boxed{\frac{5}{5}}$ $\frac{12}{5}$ $\boxed{\frac{9}{5}}$ $\frac{22}{5}$ $\boxed{\frac{19}{5}}$ $\frac{31}{5}$ $\boxed{\frac{28}{5}}$

33

(3) What fraction is $\frac{7}{8}$ less than each of these?

$\frac{8}{8}$ $\boxed{\frac{1}{8}}$ $\frac{12}{8}$ $\boxed{\frac{5}{8}}$ $\frac{20}{8}$ $\boxed{\frac{13}{8}}$ $\frac{32}{8}$ $\boxed{\frac{25}{8}}$

(4) Continue each sequence.

$\frac{20}{3}$ $\frac{17}{3}$ $\frac{14}{3}$ $\frac{11}{3}$ $\boxed{\frac{8}{3}}$ $\boxed{\frac{5}{3}}$

$\frac{18}{20}$ $\frac{16}{20}$ $\frac{14}{20}$ $\frac{12}{20}$ $\boxed{\frac{10}{20}}$ $\boxed{\frac{8}{20}}$

(5) What fraction is ...

... $\frac{3}{5}$ less than $\frac{6}{5}$? $\boxed{\frac{3}{5}}$ ... $\frac{7}{10}$ less than $\frac{15}{10}$? $\boxed{\frac{8}{10}}$

... $\frac{9}{6}$ less than $\frac{12}{6}$? $\boxed{\frac{3}{6}}$ ... $\frac{1}{2}$ less than $\frac{21}{2}$? $\boxed{\frac{20}{2}}$

(6) In a swimming class, $\frac{1}{10}$ of the students can do the breaststroke, $\frac{6}{10}$ can do the crawl and $\frac{2}{10}$ can do the butterfly stroke. The remaining students cannot swim. What fraction of the class cannot swim? $\boxed{\frac{1}{10}}$

Subtracting fractions with the same denominators should be straightforward, but a number line will help if your child encounters problems. Encourage your child to simplify any answer wherever possible.

Answers:

34–35 Comparing, ordering and simplifying
36–37 Mixed numbers and improper fractions

---

34 / 35

1) Write the fractions in order, starting with the smallest.

$\frac{1}{2}$ $\frac{2}{8}$ $\frac{3}{4}$ → $\frac{2}{8}$ $\frac{1}{2}$ $\frac{3}{4}$ $\frac{4}{3}$ $\frac{9}{12}$ $\frac{3}{6}$ → $\frac{3}{6}$ $\frac{9}{12}$ $\frac{4}{3}$

$\frac{3}{8}$ $\frac{5}{2}$ $\frac{2}{4}$ → $\frac{3}{8}$ $\frac{2}{4}$ $\frac{5}{2}$ $\frac{4}{5}$ $\frac{9}{10}$ $\frac{7}{10}$ → $\frac{7}{10}$ $\frac{4}{5}$ $\frac{9}{10}$

2) Simplify each fraction to a whole number.

$\frac{12}{6}$ = 2 $\frac{9}{3}$ = 3 $\frac{16}{2}$ = 8 $\frac{20}{10}$ = 2

$\frac{16}{4}$ = 4 $\frac{12}{3}$ = 4 $\frac{14}{7}$ = 2 $\frac{24}{6}$ = 4

$\frac{8}{2}$ = 4 $\frac{24}{2}$ = 12 $\frac{12}{2}$ = 6 $\frac{50}{2}$ = 25

$\frac{72}{4}$ = 18 $\frac{60}{5}$ = 12 $\frac{80}{4}$ = 20 $\frac{100}{5}$ = 20

$\frac{24}{3}$ = 8 $\frac{30}{6}$ = 5 $\frac{42}{7}$ = 6 $\frac{200}{10}$ = 20

3) Circle the larger fraction in each pair.

$\boxed{\frac{12}{4}}$ $\frac{4}{2}$ $\frac{18}{6}$ $\boxed{\frac{12}{3}}$ $\frac{30}{10}$ $\boxed{\frac{50}{5}}$ $\frac{48}{12}$ $\boxed{\frac{20}{4}}$

4) Circle the smallest fraction in each group.

$\frac{5}{2}$ $\frac{8}{12}$ $\boxed{\frac{2}{6}}$ $\frac{9}{4}$ $\boxed{\frac{12}{8}}$ $\frac{5}{2}$ $\frac{3}{5}$ $\frac{12}{10}$ $\boxed{\frac{1}{20}}$ $\frac{7}{8}$ $\frac{2}{4}$ $\boxed{\frac{3}{8}}$

5) Write each fraction as a mixed number.

$\frac{3}{2}$ = $1\frac{1}{2}$ $\frac{13}{4}$ = $3\frac{1}{4}$ $\frac{8}{5}$ = $1\frac{3}{5}$

$\frac{7}{2}$ = $3\frac{1}{2}$ $\frac{15}{2}$ = $7\frac{1}{2}$ $\frac{27}{4}$ = $6\frac{3}{4}$

$\frac{19}{3}$ = $6\frac{1}{3}$ $\frac{38}{5}$ = $7\frac{3}{5}$ $\frac{51}{7}$ = $7\frac{2}{7}$

Success with this work requires your child to "see" connections between the denominators to find a common one. For example, $\frac{1}{2}$ and $\frac{1}{4}$ have "4" as a common denominator.

---

36 / 37

1) Convert each mixed number to an improper fraction.

$3\frac{1}{2}$ = $\frac{7}{2}$ $5\frac{1}{3}$ = $\frac{16}{3}$ $7\frac{7}{10}$ = $\frac{77}{10}$ $7\frac{2}{5}$ = $\frac{37}{5}$

$3\frac{1}{10}$ = $\frac{31}{10}$ $5\frac{1}{2}$ = $\frac{11}{2}$ $8\frac{7}{8}$ = $\frac{71}{8}$ $6\frac{2}{5}$ = $\frac{32}{5}$

$8\frac{7}{10}$ = $\frac{87}{10}$ $4\frac{5}{6}$ = $\frac{29}{6}$ $3\frac{9}{10}$ = $\frac{39}{10}$ $3\frac{3}{8}$ = $\frac{27}{8}$

$1\frac{1}{10}$ = $\frac{11}{10}$ $4\frac{4}{5}$ = $\frac{24}{5}$ $2\frac{7}{9}$ = $\frac{25}{9}$ $10\frac{5}{6}$ = $\frac{65}{6}$

$10\frac{3}{4}$ = $\frac{43}{4}$ $5\frac{1}{8}$ = $\frac{41}{8}$ $6\frac{3}{5}$ = $\frac{33}{5}$ $12\frac{1}{2}$ = $\frac{25}{2}$

$11\frac{4}{7}$ = $\frac{81}{7}$ $5\frac{3}{4}$ = $\frac{23}{4}$ $2\frac{3}{5}$ = $\frac{13}{5}$ $6\frac{5}{8}$ = $\frac{53}{8}$

2) Write each improper fraction as a mixed number.

$\frac{14}{3}$ = $4\frac{2}{3}$ $\frac{27}{2}$ = $13\frac{1}{2}$ $\frac{16}{5}$ = $3\frac{1}{5}$

$\frac{26}{10}$ = $2\frac{6}{10}$ $\frac{19}{4}$ = $4\frac{3}{4}$ $\frac{12}{10}$ = $1\frac{2}{10}$

$\frac{13}{3}$ = $4\frac{1}{3}$ $\frac{32}{10}$ = $3\frac{2}{10}$ $\frac{15}{9}$ = $1\frac{6}{9}$

$\frac{13}{12}$ = $1\frac{1}{12}$ $\frac{42}{10}$ = $4\frac{2}{10}$ $\frac{81}{2}$ = $40\frac{1}{2}$

$\frac{29}{4}$ = $7\frac{1}{4}$ $\frac{62}{5}$ = $12\frac{2}{5}$ $\frac{67}{11}$ = $6\frac{1}{11}$

$\frac{39}{12}$ = $3\frac{3}{12}$ $\frac{30}{7}$ = $4\frac{2}{7}$ $\frac{50}{20}$ = $2\frac{10}{20}$

Mixed numbers, sometimes known as mixed fractions, are common in maths and your child needs to be able to convert them into improper fractions, or top-heavy fractions, and vice versa.

Answers:

38–39 Adding, subtracting and simplifying
40–41 Beat the clock 2, see p.80
42–43 Multiplying fractions 1

38

① Write the answers as mixed numbers.

$\frac{2}{3} + \frac{2}{3} = 1\frac{1}{3}$ $\frac{3}{4} + \frac{2}{4} = 1\frac{1}{4}$ $\frac{4}{5} + \frac{4}{5} = 1\frac{3}{5}$

$\frac{6}{7} + \frac{4}{7} = 1\frac{3}{7}$ $\frac{5}{6} + \frac{4}{6} = 1\frac{3}{6}$ $\frac{7}{8} + \frac{3}{8} = 1\frac{2}{8}$

$\frac{9}{10} + \frac{3}{10} = 1\frac{2}{10}$ $\frac{7}{10} + \frac{6}{10} = 1\frac{3}{10}$ $\frac{9}{15} + \frac{16}{15} = 1\frac{10}{15}$

② Do the subtraction and simplify the answer.

$\frac{9}{10} - \frac{4}{10} = \frac{5}{10} = \frac{1}{2}$ $\frac{7}{15} - \frac{4}{15} = \frac{3}{15} = \frac{1}{5}$ $\frac{20}{25} - \frac{5}{25} = \frac{15}{25} = \frac{3}{5}$

$\frac{17}{30} - \frac{9}{30} = \frac{8}{30} = \frac{4}{15}$ $\frac{11}{20} - \frac{6}{20} = \frac{5}{20} = \frac{1}{4}$ $\frac{8}{15} - \frac{3}{15} = \frac{5}{15} = \frac{1}{3}$

39

③ Write the answers as mixed numbers.

$2\frac{3}{5} + 4\frac{1}{5} = 6\frac{4}{5}$ $3\frac{1}{4} + 4\frac{1}{4} = 7\frac{2}{4}$

$3\frac{3}{10} + 4\frac{1}{10} = 7\frac{4}{10}$ $8\frac{2}{5} + 3\frac{4}{5} = 12\frac{1}{5}$

$6\frac{1}{4} + 2\frac{1}{4} + 4\frac{1}{4} = 12\frac{3}{4}$ $12\frac{1}{2} + 3\frac{1}{2} + 4\frac{1}{2} = 20\frac{1}{2}$

④ Write the answers as mixed numbers.

$6 - 3\frac{3}{4} = 2\frac{1}{4}$ $2\frac{2}{3} - 1 = 1\frac{2}{3}$ $7 - 1\frac{4}{5} = 5\frac{1}{5}$

$4 - 1\frac{1}{3} = 2\frac{2}{3}$ $5\frac{1}{2} - 3 = 2\frac{1}{2}$ $6 - 1\frac{2}{10} = 4\frac{8}{10}$

$7 - 1\frac{1}{6} = 5\frac{5}{6}$ $3\frac{1}{2} - 2 = 1\frac{1}{2}$ $8 - 6\frac{1}{4} = 1\frac{3}{4}$

This work is an extension of previous problems and the key to crack it is to simplify the answers wherever possible. At this point, your child may be so keen to complete the work that he or she misreads the operation symbol and adds instead of subtracting or vice versa!

42

① Multiply each fraction by 4.

$\frac{1}{2}$ 2 $\frac{1}{4}$ 1 $\frac{1}{5}$ $\frac{4}{5}$ $\frac{1}{10}$ $\frac{4}{10}$

② Multiply each fraction by 7.

$\frac{1}{2}$ $\frac{7}{2}$ $\frac{1}{3}$ $\frac{7}{3}$ $\frac{1}{10}$ $\frac{7}{10}$ $\frac{1}{4}$ $\frac{7}{4}$

③ Multiply each fraction by 10.

$\frac{1}{2}$ 5 $\frac{1}{5}$ 2 $\frac{1}{4}$ $\frac{10}{4}$ $\frac{1}{6}$ $\frac{10}{6}$

④ Multiply each fraction by 6.

$\frac{1}{6}$ 1 $\frac{1}{4}$ $\frac{6}{4}$ $\frac{1}{10}$ $\frac{6}{10}$ $\frac{1}{12}$ $\frac{6}{12}$

⑤ Multiply each number by $\frac{1}{2}$.

6 3   12 6   1 $\frac{1}{2}$ 20 10

⑥ Multiply each number by $\frac{1}{4}$.

12 3   24 6   40 10   100 25

43

⑦ Multiply each number by $\frac{1}{5}$ and write the answer as an improper fraction and then as a mixed number.

6 $\frac{6}{5}$ = $1\frac{1}{5}$ 18 $\frac{18}{5}$ = $3\frac{3}{5}$ 24 $\frac{24}{5}$ = $4\frac{4}{5}$

⑧ Multiply each number by $\frac{1}{10}$ and write the answer as an improper fraction and then as a mixed number.

15 $\frac{15}{10}$ = $1\frac{5}{10}$ 24 $\frac{24}{10}$ = $2\frac{4}{10}$ 45 $\frac{45}{10}$ = $4\frac{5}{10}$

⑨ Multiply each fraction by 7 and write the answer as an improper fraction and then as a mixed number.

$\frac{1}{3}$ $\frac{7}{3}$ = $2\frac{1}{3}$ $\frac{1}{4}$ $\frac{7}{4}$ = $1\frac{3}{4}$ $\frac{1}{5}$ $\frac{7}{5}$ = $1\frac{2}{5}$

⑩ Mrs Brown buys some lemonade for a school picnic. Ten children drink a quarter of a bottle each. How many bottles do the children drink altogether? Give your answer as a mixed number.

$2\frac{1}{2}$

Although your child will eventually learn to multiply the numerator by the whole number, he or she may often forget to simplify the result after that.

Your child may also need to change an improper fraction into a mixed number.

Answers:

44–45 Multiplying fractions 2
46–47 Multiplying and simplifying

44

(1) Multiply each fraction by 8 and write the answer as an improper fraction and then as a mixed number.

$\frac{1}{3}$ | $\frac{8}{3}$ | = $2\frac{2}{3}$ $\frac{3}{7}$ | $\frac{24}{7}$ | = $3\frac{3}{7}$ $\frac{4}{5}$ | $\frac{32}{5}$ | = $6\frac{2}{5}$

(2) Multiply each fraction by 4 and write the answer as an improper fraction and then as a mixed number.

$\frac{2}{5}$ | $\frac{8}{5}$ | = $1\frac{3}{5}$ $\frac{2}{3}$ | $\frac{8}{3}$ | = $2\frac{2}{3}$ $\frac{3}{5}$ | $\frac{12}{5}$ | = $2\frac{2}{5}$

(3) Multiply each fraction by 6 and write the answer as an improper fraction and then as a mixed number.

$\frac{3}{4}$ | $\frac{18}{4}$ | = $4\frac{2}{4}$ $\frac{4}{5}$ | $\frac{24}{5}$ | = $4\frac{4}{5}$ $\frac{2}{7}$ | $\frac{12}{7}$ | = $1\frac{5}{7}$

(4) Multiply each fraction by 12 and write the answer as an improper fraction and then as a mixed number.

$\frac{3}{7}$ | $\frac{36}{7}$ | = $5\frac{1}{7}$ $\frac{2}{5}$ | $\frac{24}{5}$ | = $4\frac{4}{5}$ $\frac{6}{10}$ | $\frac{72}{10}$ | = $7\frac{2}{10}$

(5) Multiply each fraction by 10 and write the answer as an improper fraction and then as a mixed number.

$\frac{7}{12}$ | $\frac{70}{12}$ | = $5\frac{10}{12}$ $\frac{4}{3}$ | $\frac{40}{3}$ | = $13\frac{1}{3}$ $\frac{5}{6}$ | $\frac{50}{6}$ | = $8\frac{2}{6}$

45

(6) Multiply each number by $\frac{1}{4}$ and simplify the answer.

24 | $\frac{24}{4}$ | = 6   40 | $\frac{40}{4}$ | = 10   32 | $\frac{32}{4}$ | = 8

(7) Multiply each number by $\frac{3}{5}$ and write the answer as an improper fraction and then as a mixed number.

12 | $\frac{36}{5}$ | = $7\frac{1}{5}$ 16 | $\frac{48}{5}$ | = $9\frac{3}{5}$ 21 | $\frac{63}{5}$ | = $12\frac{3}{5}$

(8) Multiply each number by $\frac{3}{4}$ and write the answer as an improper fraction and then as a mixed number.

15 | $\frac{45}{4}$ | = $11\frac{1}{4}$ 21 | $\frac{63}{4}$ | = $15\frac{3}{4}$ 26 | $\frac{78}{4}$ | = $19\frac{2}{4}$

(9) Multiply each fraction by 9 and write the answer as an improper fraction and then as a mixed number.

$\frac{2}{7}$ | $\frac{18}{7}$ | = $2\frac{4}{7}$ $\frac{3}{4}$ | $\frac{27}{4}$ | = $6\frac{3}{4}$ $\frac{4}{5}$ | $\frac{36}{5}$ | = $7\frac{1}{5}$

(10) Multiply each fraction by 11 and write the answer as an improper fraction and then as a mixed number.

$\frac{3}{4}$ | $\frac{33}{4}$ | = $8\frac{1}{4}$ $\frac{5}{7}$ | $\frac{55}{7}$ | = $7\frac{6}{7}$ $\frac{3}{8}$ | $\frac{33}{8}$ | = $4\frac{1}{8}$

These questions follow on from the previous pages and require your child to work with slightly more difficult examples and larger numbers with larger fractions.

Always encourage your child to convert improper fractions into mixed numbers and to simplify the answers wherever possible.

46

(1) Multiply the fractions.

$\frac{1}{2} \times \frac{1}{3} = \frac{1}{6}$ $\frac{1}{2} \times \frac{1}{4} = \frac{1}{8}$ $\frac{1}{5} \times \frac{1}{2} = \frac{1}{10}$

$\frac{1}{10} \times \frac{1}{2} = \frac{1}{20}$ $\frac{1}{5} \times \frac{2}{3} = \frac{2}{15}$ $\frac{3}{4} \times \frac{1}{2} = \frac{3}{8}$

(2) Multiply the fractions and simplify the answers.

$\frac{6}{10} \times \frac{2}{3} = \frac{2}{5}$ $\frac{3}{5} \times \frac{5}{8} = \frac{3}{8}$ $\frac{3}{4} \times \frac{5}{6} = \frac{5}{8}$

$\frac{1}{4} \times \frac{2}{3} = \frac{1}{6}$ $\frac{1}{4} \times \frac{4}{7} = \frac{1}{7}$ $\frac{3}{10} \times \frac{5}{7} = \frac{3}{14}$

$\frac{1}{3} \times \frac{3}{5} = \frac{1}{5}$ $\frac{3}{8} \times \frac{2}{3} = \frac{1}{4}$ $\frac{1}{10} \times \frac{2}{3} = \frac{1}{15}$

47

(3) Multiply the fractions. Write the answer in its simplest form.

$\frac{1}{10} \times \frac{1}{5} = \frac{1}{50}$ $\frac{2}{5} \times \frac{2}{10} = \frac{2}{25}$ $\frac{1}{12} \times \frac{2}{3} = \frac{1}{18}$

$\frac{2}{12} \times \frac{3}{4} = \frac{1}{8}$ $\frac{3}{12} \times \frac{3}{4} = \frac{3}{16}$ $\frac{5}{12} \times \frac{2}{3} = \frac{5}{18}$

$\frac{6}{12} \times \frac{5}{10} = \frac{1}{4}$ $\frac{3}{4} \times \frac{6}{8} = \frac{9}{16}$ $\frac{1}{2} \times \frac{1}{3} \times \frac{1}{4} = \frac{1}{24}$

$\frac{1}{3} \times \frac{1}{5} \times \frac{1}{10} = \frac{1}{150}$ $\frac{1}{4} \times \frac{1}{2} \times \frac{3}{4} = \frac{3}{32}$ $\frac{1}{3} \times \frac{2}{3} \times \frac{1}{4} = \frac{1}{18}$

$\frac{1}{5} \times \frac{1}{3} \times \frac{1}{10} = \frac{1}{150}$ $\frac{1}{5} \times \frac{2}{3} \times \frac{1}{10} = \frac{1}{75}$ $\frac{1}{5} \times \frac{2}{5} \times \frac{3}{5} = \frac{6}{125}$

$\frac{1}{4} \times \frac{2}{4} \times \frac{3}{4} = \frac{3}{32}$ $\frac{7}{12} \times \frac{1}{2} \times \frac{8}{10} = \frac{7}{30}$ $\frac{3}{4} \times \frac{4}{5} \times \frac{5}{6} = \frac{1}{2}$

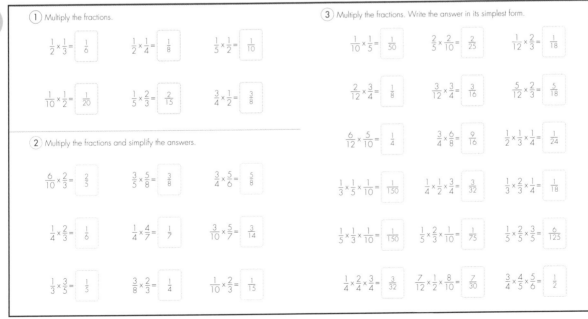

Your child will probably have been taught to "multiply the top by the top and the bottom by the bottom". Make sure they simplify the answer wherever possible. It is good to show your child ways to "cancel" some fractions wherever possible before multiplying. Doing that can reduce the size of numbers in the calculation. For example: $\frac{98}{196} \times \frac{350}{700}$ is the same as $\frac{1}{2} \times \frac{1}{2}$!

Answers:

48–49 Dividing fractions
50–51 Multiplying and dividing fractions

48 | **49**

① Divide the fractions by the whole numbers. Simplify any answers you can.

$\frac{1}{3} \div 2 = \boxed{\frac{1}{6}}$ $\qquad$ $\frac{1}{4} \div 3 = \boxed{\frac{1}{12}}$ $\qquad$ $\frac{1}{5} \div 2 = \boxed{\frac{1}{10}}$

$\frac{1}{10} \div 4 = \boxed{\frac{1}{40}}$ $\qquad$ $\frac{2}{3} \div 2 = \boxed{\frac{1}{3}}$ $\qquad$ $\frac{3}{4} \div 2 = \boxed{\frac{3}{8}}$

$\frac{3}{5} \div 3 = \boxed{\frac{1}{5}}$ $\qquad$ $\frac{1}{10} \div 3 = \boxed{\frac{1}{30}}$ $\qquad$ $\frac{1}{2} \div 10 = \boxed{\frac{1}{20}}$

$\frac{1}{3} \div 8 = \boxed{\frac{1}{24}}$ $\qquad$ $\frac{1}{10} \div 7 = \boxed{\frac{1}{70}}$ $\qquad$ $\frac{2}{3} \div 4 = \boxed{\frac{1}{6}}$

$\frac{4}{5} \div 3 = \boxed{\frac{4}{15}}$ $\qquad$ $\frac{3}{4} \div 6 = \boxed{\frac{1}{8}}$ $\qquad$ $\frac{5}{8} \div 10 = \boxed{\frac{1}{16}}$

$\frac{4}{5} \div 4 = \boxed{\frac{1}{5}}$ $\qquad$ $\frac{2}{3} \div 12 = \boxed{\frac{1}{18}}$ $\qquad$ $\frac{5}{6} \div 10 = \boxed{\frac{1}{12}}$

② Write down the answers in their simplest form.

$\frac{4}{9} \div 8 = \boxed{\frac{1}{18}}$ $\qquad$ $\frac{7}{8} \div 7 = \boxed{\frac{1}{8}}$ $\qquad$ $\frac{8}{9} \div 4 = \boxed{\frac{2}{9}}$

$\frac{5}{7} \div 5 = \boxed{\frac{1}{7}}$ $\qquad$ $\frac{4}{10} \div 4 = \boxed{\frac{1}{10}}$ $\qquad$ $\frac{5}{9} \div 10 = \boxed{\frac{1}{18}}$

$\frac{6}{7} \div 12 = \boxed{\frac{1}{14}}$ $\qquad$ $\frac{4}{5} \div 12 = \boxed{\frac{1}{15}}$ $\qquad$ $\frac{8}{12} \div 8 = \boxed{\frac{1}{12}}$

$\frac{3}{7} \div 12 = \boxed{\frac{1}{28}}$ $\qquad$ $\frac{6}{10} \div 4 = \boxed{\frac{3}{20}}$ $\qquad$ $\frac{6}{7} \div 10 = \boxed{\frac{3}{35}}$

③ Pete has £10. He gives four-fifths ($\frac{4}{5}$) of it to his four children to share equally between them on rides at a fun fair. How much does each child have to spend?

$\boxed{£2}$

Your child should have an understanding that dividing by a whole number is the same as multiplying by the unitary fraction of that number. For example: dividing by 9 is the same as multiplying by $\frac{1}{9}$. Encourage simplification of the answer wherever possible.

50 | **51**

① Multiply each fraction by 8. Write the answer as an improper fraction and then as a mixed number.

$\frac{4}{7}$ $\boxed{\frac{32}{7}}$ = $\boxed{4\frac{4}{7}}$ $\qquad$ $\frac{8}{9}$ $\boxed{\frac{64}{9}}$ = $\boxed{7\frac{1}{9}}$ $\qquad$ $\frac{4}{11}$ $\boxed{\frac{32}{11}}$ = $\boxed{2\frac{10}{11}}$

② Multiply each fraction by 15. Write the answer as an improper fraction and then as a mixed or whole number.

$\frac{1}{4}$ $\boxed{\frac{15}{4}}$ = $\boxed{3\frac{3}{4}}$ $\qquad$ $\frac{2}{10}$ $\boxed{\frac{30}{10}}$ = $\boxed{3}$ $\qquad$ $\frac{4}{5}$ $\boxed{\frac{60}{5}}$ = $\boxed{12}$

③ Multiply each fraction by 20. Write the answer as an improper fraction and then as a mixed number.

$\frac{5}{6}$ $\boxed{\frac{100}{6}}$ = $\boxed{16\frac{4}{6}}$ $\qquad$ $\frac{8}{12}$ $\boxed{\frac{160}{12}}$ = $\boxed{13\frac{4}{12}}$ $\qquad$ $\frac{6}{7}$ $\boxed{\frac{120}{7}}$ = $\boxed{17\frac{1}{7}}$

④ Multiply each mixed number by 4. Simplify any answers you can.

$4\frac{1}{8}$ $\boxed{16\frac{1}{2}}$ $\qquad$ $2\frac{1}{4}$ $\boxed{9}$ $\qquad$ $3\frac{3}{4}$ $\boxed{15}$ $\qquad$ $1\frac{1}{2}$ $\boxed{6}$

⑤ Multiply each mixed number by 10. Simplify any answers you can.

$4\frac{1}{2}$ $\boxed{45}$ $\qquad$ $5\frac{2}{5}$ $\boxed{54}$ $\qquad$ $7\frac{1}{4}$ $\boxed{72\frac{1}{2}}$ $\qquad$ $10\frac{1}{10}$ $\boxed{101}$

⑥ Divide each whole number by 3 and write the answer as a mixed number.

10 $\boxed{3\frac{1}{3}}$ $\qquad$ 14 $\boxed{4\frac{2}{3}}$ $\qquad$ 20 $\boxed{6\frac{2}{3}}$ $\qquad$ 28 $\boxed{9\frac{1}{3}}$

⑦ Divide each whole number by 5 and write the answer as a mixed number.

18 $\boxed{3\frac{3}{5}}$ $\qquad$ 27 $\boxed{5\frac{2}{5}}$ $\qquad$ 43 $\boxed{8\frac{3}{5}}$ $\qquad$ 61 $\boxed{12\frac{1}{5}}$

⑧ Divide each whole number by 7 and write the answer as a mixed number.

9 $\boxed{1\frac{2}{7}}$ $\qquad$ 18 $\boxed{2\frac{4}{7}}$ $\qquad$ 45 $\boxed{6\frac{3}{7}}$ $\qquad$ 67 $\boxed{9\frac{4}{7}}$

⑨ Divide each whole number by 8 and write the answer as a mixed number.

23 $\boxed{2\frac{7}{8}}$ $\qquad$ 41 $\boxed{5\frac{1}{8}}$ $\qquad$ 9 $\boxed{1\frac{1}{8}}$ $\qquad$ 45 $\boxed{5\frac{5}{8}}$

⑩ Divide each whole number by 10 and write the answer as a mixed number.

15 $\boxed{1\frac{1}{2}}$ $\qquad$ 23 $\boxed{2\frac{3}{10}}$ $\qquad$ 56 $\boxed{5\frac{3}{5}}$ $\qquad$ 77 $\boxed{7\frac{7}{10}}$

Your child may have been taught at least two different ways of working out these types of sums, so a judgment call may be needed depending on their success. If he or she is confident and successful with one method, let him or her continue. If he or she is struggling, offer help with another method or speak to the teacher.

Answers:

52–53 Common denomiators
54–55 Comparing fractions

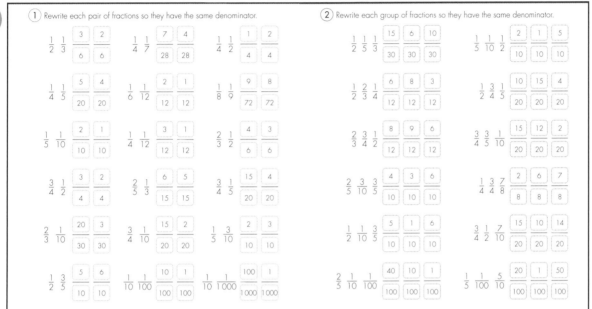

52

(1) Rewrite each pair of fractions so they have the same denominator.

$\frac{1}{2}$ $\frac{1}{3}$ → $\frac{3}{6}$ $\frac{2}{6}$ $\frac{1}{4}$ $\frac{1}{7}$ → $\frac{7}{28}$ $\frac{4}{28}$ $\frac{1}{4}$ $\frac{1}{2}$ → $\frac{1}{4}$ $\frac{2}{4}$

$\frac{1}{4}$ $\frac{1}{5}$ → $\frac{5}{20}$ $\frac{4}{20}$ $\frac{1}{6}$ $\frac{1}{12}$ → $\frac{2}{12}$ $\frac{1}{12}$ $\frac{1}{8}$ $\frac{1}{9}$ → $\frac{9}{72}$ $\frac{8}{72}$

$\frac{1}{5}$ $\frac{1}{10}$ → $\frac{2}{10}$ $\frac{1}{10}$ $\frac{1}{4}$ $\frac{1}{12}$ → $\frac{3}{12}$ $\frac{1}{12}$ $\frac{2}{3}$ $\frac{1}{2}$ → $\frac{4}{6}$ $\frac{3}{6}$

$\frac{3}{4}$ $\frac{1}{2}$ → $\frac{3}{4}$ $\frac{2}{4}$ $\frac{2}{5}$ $\frac{1}{3}$ → $\frac{6}{15}$ $\frac{5}{15}$ $\frac{3}{4}$ $\frac{1}{5}$ → $\frac{15}{20}$ $\frac{4}{20}$

$\frac{2}{3}$ $\frac{1}{10}$ → $\frac{20}{30}$ $\frac{3}{30}$ $\frac{3}{4}$ $\frac{1}{10}$ → $\frac{15}{20}$ $\frac{2}{20}$ $\frac{1}{5}$ $\frac{3}{10}$ → $\frac{2}{10}$ $\frac{3}{10}$

$\frac{1}{2}$ $\frac{3}{5}$ → $\frac{5}{10}$ $\frac{6}{10}$ $\frac{1}{10}$ $\frac{1}{100}$ → $\frac{10}{100}$ $\frac{1}{100}$ $\frac{1}{10}$ $\frac{1}{1000}$ → $\frac{100}{1000}$ $\frac{1}{1000}$

Recognising a "common" number that both denominators can "go into" requires good knowledge of times tables. For example: the common denominator of $\frac{1}{6}$ and $\frac{1}{7}$ is 42.

53

(2) Rewrite each group of fractions so they have the same denominator.

$\frac{1}{2}$ $\frac{1}{5}$ $\frac{1}{3}$ → $\frac{15}{30}$ $\frac{6}{30}$ $\frac{10}{30}$ $\frac{1}{5}$ $\frac{1}{10}$ $\frac{1}{2}$ → $\frac{2}{10}$ $\frac{1}{10}$ $\frac{5}{10}$

$\frac{1}{2}$ $\frac{2}{3}$ $\frac{1}{4}$ → $\frac{6}{12}$ $\frac{8}{12}$ $\frac{3}{12}$ $\frac{1}{2}$ $\frac{3}{4}$ $\frac{1}{5}$ → $\frac{10}{20}$ $\frac{15}{20}$ $\frac{4}{20}$

$\frac{2}{3}$ $\frac{3}{4}$ $\frac{1}{2}$ → $\frac{8}{12}$ $\frac{9}{12}$ $\frac{6}{12}$ $\frac{3}{4}$ $\frac{3}{5}$ $\frac{1}{10}$ → $\frac{15}{20}$ $\frac{12}{20}$ $\frac{2}{20}$

$\frac{2}{5}$ $\frac{3}{10}$ $\frac{3}{5}$ → $\frac{4}{10}$ $\frac{3}{10}$ $\frac{6}{10}$ $\frac{1}{4}$ $\frac{3}{4}$ $\frac{7}{8}$ → $\frac{2}{8}$ $\frac{6}{8}$ $\frac{7}{8}$

$\frac{1}{2}$ $\frac{1}{10}$ $\frac{3}{5}$ → $\frac{5}{10}$ $\frac{1}{10}$ $\frac{6}{10}$ $\frac{3}{4}$ $\frac{1}{2}$ $\frac{7}{10}$ → $\frac{15}{20}$ $\frac{10}{20}$ $\frac{14}{20}$

$\frac{2}{5}$ $\frac{1}{10}$ $\frac{1}{100}$ → $\frac{40}{100}$ $\frac{10}{100}$ $\frac{1}{100}$ $\frac{1}{5}$ $\frac{1}{100}$ $\frac{5}{10}$ → $\frac{20}{100}$ $\frac{1}{100}$ $\frac{50}{100}$

Your child should be encouraged to look for the smallest common denominator. For example: $\frac{1}{12}$ and $\frac{1}{6}$ could be 72, but in fact 12 would do the job!

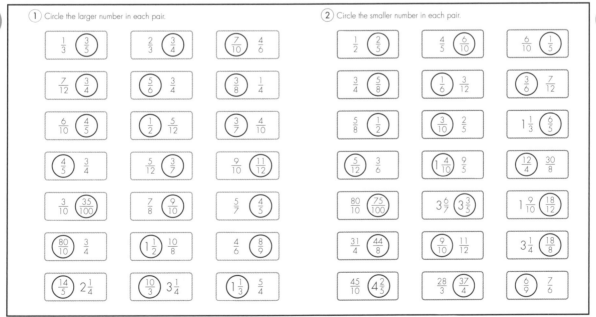

54

(1) Circle the larger number in each pair.

$\frac{1}{3}$ (⭕$\frac{3}{5}$) $\frac{2}{3}$ (⭕$\frac{3}{4}$)   (⭕$\frac{7}{10}$) $\frac{4}{6}$

(⭕$\frac{7}{12}$) $\frac{3}{4}$ $\frac{5}{6}$ (⭕) $\frac{3}{4}$ (⭕$\frac{3}{8}$) $\frac{1}{4}$

$\frac{6}{10}$ (⭕$\frac{4}{5}$)   (⭕$\frac{1}{2}$) $\frac{5}{12}$ $\frac{3}{7}$ (⭕$\frac{4}{10}$)

(⭕$\frac{4}{5}$) $\frac{3}{4}$ $\frac{5}{12}$ (⭕$\frac{3}{7}$) $\frac{9}{10}$ (⭕$\frac{11}{12}$)

$\frac{3}{10}$ (⭕$\frac{35}{100}$) $\frac{7}{8}$ (⭕$\frac{9}{10}$) $\frac{5}{7}$ (⭕$\frac{4}{5}$)

(⭕$\frac{80}{10}$) $\frac{3}{4}$ (⭕$1\frac{1}{2}$) $\frac{10}{8}$ $\frac{4}{6}$ (⭕$\frac{8}{9}$)

(⭕$\frac{14}{5}$) $2\frac{1}{4}$ (⭕$\frac{10}{3}$) $3\frac{1}{4}$ (⭕$1\frac{1}{3}$) $\frac{5}{4}$

This work extends what is covered in previous pages. The exercises become more complicated, however, because they may require your child to change

55

(2) Circle the smaller number in each pair.

$\frac{1}{2}$ (⭕$\frac{2}{5}$) $\frac{4}{5}$ (⭕$\frac{6}{10}$) $\frac{6}{10}$ (⭕$\frac{1}{5}$)

$\frac{3}{4}$ (⭕$\frac{5}{8}$)   (⭕$\frac{1}{6}$) $\frac{3}{12}$ (⭕$\frac{3}{6}$) $\frac{7}{12}$

$\frac{5}{8}$ (⭕$\frac{1}{2}$)   (⭕$\frac{3}{10}$) $\frac{2}{5}$ $1\frac{1}{3}$ (⭕$\frac{6}{5}$)

(⭕$\frac{5}{12}$) $\frac{3}{6}$ (⭕$1\frac{4}{10}$) $\frac{9}{5}$ (⭕$\frac{12}{4}$) $\frac{30}{8}$

$\frac{80}{10}$ (⭕$\frac{75}{100}$) $3\frac{6}{7}$ (⭕$3\frac{3}{5}$) $1\frac{9}{10}$ (⭕$\frac{18}{12}$)

$\frac{31}{4}$ (⭕$\frac{44}{8}$)   (⭕$\frac{9}{10}$) $\frac{11}{12}$ $3\frac{1}{4}$ (⭕$\frac{18}{8}$)

$\frac{45}{10}$ (⭕$4\frac{2}{5}$) $\frac{28}{3}$ (⭕$\frac{37}{4}$)   (⭕$\frac{6}{9}$) $\frac{7}{6}$

a mixed number into an improper fraction before moving on to the next stage of the comparison.

Answers:

56–57 More adding and subtracting
58–59 Fractions and decimals

56 / **57**

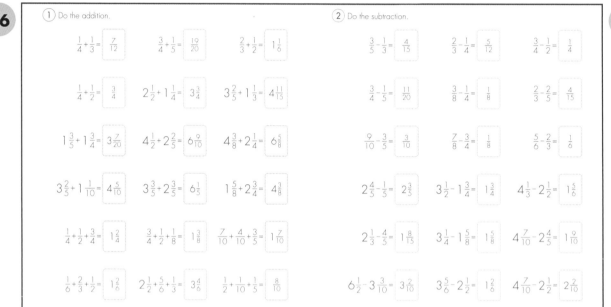

① Do the addition.

$\frac{1}{4}+\frac{1}{3}=\frac{7}{12}$ $\frac{3}{4}+\frac{1}{5}=\frac{19}{20}$ $\frac{2}{3}+\frac{1}{2}=1\frac{1}{6}$

$\frac{1}{4}+\frac{1}{2}=\frac{3}{4}$ $2\frac{1}{2}+1\frac{1}{4}=3\frac{3}{4}$ $3\frac{2}{5}+1\frac{1}{3}=4\frac{11}{15}$

$1\frac{3}{5}+1\frac{3}{4}=3\frac{7}{20}$ $4\frac{1}{2}+2\frac{2}{5}=6\frac{9}{10}$ $4\frac{3}{8}+2\frac{1}{4}=6\frac{5}{8}$

$3\frac{2}{5}+1\frac{1}{10}=4\frac{5}{10}$ $3\frac{3}{5}+2\frac{3}{5}=6\frac{1}{5}$ $1\frac{5}{8}+2\frac{3}{4}=4\frac{3}{8}$

$\frac{1}{4}+\frac{1}{2}+\frac{3}{4}=1\frac{2}{4}$ $\frac{3}{4}+\frac{1}{2}+\frac{1}{8}=1\frac{3}{8}$ $\frac{7}{10}+\frac{4}{10}+\frac{3}{5}=1\frac{7}{10}$

$\frac{1}{6}+\frac{2}{3}+\frac{1}{2}=1\frac{2}{6}$ $2\frac{1}{2}+\frac{5}{6}+\frac{1}{3}=3\frac{4}{6}$ $\frac{1}{2}+\frac{1}{10}+\frac{1}{5}=\frac{8}{10}$

② Do the subtraction.

$\frac{3}{5}-\frac{1}{3}=\frac{4}{15}$ $\frac{2}{3}-\frac{1}{4}=\frac{5}{12}$ $\frac{3}{4}-\frac{1}{2}=\frac{1}{4}$

$\frac{3}{4}-\frac{1}{5}=\frac{11}{20}$ $\frac{3}{8}-\frac{1}{4}=\frac{1}{8}$ $\frac{2}{3}-\frac{2}{5}=\frac{4}{15}$

$\frac{9}{10}-\frac{3}{5}=\frac{3}{10}$ $\frac{7}{8}-\frac{3}{4}=\frac{1}{8}$ $\frac{5}{6}-\frac{2}{3}=\frac{1}{6}$

$2\frac{4}{5}-\frac{1}{5}=2\frac{3}{5}$ $3\frac{1}{2}-1\frac{3}{4}=1\frac{3}{4}$ $4\frac{1}{3}-2\frac{1}{2}=1\frac{5}{6}$

$2\frac{1}{3}-\frac{4}{5}=1\frac{8}{15}$ $3\frac{1}{4}-1\frac{5}{8}=1\frac{5}{8}$ $4\frac{7}{10}-2\frac{4}{5}=1\frac{9}{10}$

$6\frac{1}{2}-3\frac{3}{10}=3\frac{2}{10}$ $3\frac{5}{6}-2\frac{1}{2}=1\frac{2}{6}$ $4\frac{7}{10}-2\frac{1}{2}=2\frac{2}{10}$

This work continues with the practice of addition with fractions. Your child may have been taught to either convert all mixed numbers to improper fractions before adding or to add whole numbers first and then calculate the fractional part and put the two together. Whichever the method, the more practice he or she gets, the better.

58 / **59**

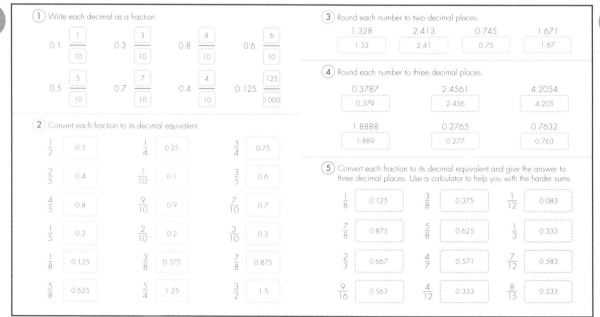

① Write each decimal as a fraction.

0.1 $\frac{1}{10}$ 0.3 $\frac{3}{10}$ 0.8 $\frac{8}{10}$ 0.6 $\frac{6}{10}$

0.5 $\frac{5}{10}$ 0.7 $\frac{7}{10}$ 0.4 $\frac{4}{10}$ 0.125 $\frac{125}{1000}$

② Convert each fraction to its decimal equivalent.

$\frac{1}{2}$ 0.5 $\frac{1}{4}$ 0.25 $\frac{3}{4}$ 0.75

$\frac{2}{5}$ 0.4 $\frac{1}{10}$ 0.1 $\frac{3}{5}$ 0.6

$\frac{4}{5}$ 0.8 $\frac{9}{10}$ 0.9 $\frac{7}{10}$ 0.7

$\frac{1}{5}$ 0.2 $\frac{2}{10}$ 0.2 $\frac{3}{10}$ 0.3

$\frac{1}{8}$ 0.125 $\frac{3}{8}$ 0.375 $\frac{7}{8}$ 0.875

$\frac{5}{8}$ 0.625 $\frac{5}{4}$ 1.25 $\frac{3}{2}$ 1.5

③ Round each number to two decimal places.

1.328   2.413   0.745   1.671
1.33   2.41   0.75   1.67

④ Round each number to three decimal places.

0.3787   2.4561   4.2054
0.379   2.456   4.205

1.8888   0.2765   0.7632
1.889   0.277   0.763

⑤ Convert each fraction to its decimal equivalent and give the answer to three decimal places. Use a calculator to help you with the harder sums.

$\frac{1}{8}$ 0.125 $\frac{3}{8}$ 0.375 $\frac{1}{12}$ 0.083

$\frac{7}{8}$ 0.875 $\frac{5}{8}$ 0.625 $\frac{1}{3}$ 0.333

$\frac{2}{3}$ 0.667 $\frac{4}{7}$ 0.571 $\frac{7}{12}$ 0.583

$\frac{9}{16}$ 0.563 $\frac{4}{12}$ 0.333 $\frac{8}{15}$ 0.533

Your child must understand the connection between fractions and their decimal equivalents, especially the simpler ones such as $\frac{1}{2}$ and 0.5, and $\frac{1}{10}$ and 0.1.

Drawing a simple number line and placing fractions above the line and the decimal equivalents below can help reinforce the idea of their connection.

Answers:

60–61 Fractions and percentages 1
62–63 Fractions and percentages 2
64–65 Beat the clock 3, see p.80

60 **61**

① Write each percentage as a fraction in its simplest form.

50% $\frac{1}{2}$ 20% $\frac{1}{5}$ 70% $\frac{7}{10}$ 10% $\frac{1}{10}$

25% $\frac{1}{4}$ 75% $\frac{3}{4}$ 5% $\frac{1}{20}$ 85% $\frac{17}{20}$

80% $\frac{4}{5}$ 35% $\frac{7}{20}$ 48% $\frac{12}{25}$ 18% $\frac{9}{50}$

② Write each fraction as a percentage.

$\frac{8}{50}$ 16% $\frac{34}{50}$ 68% $\frac{42}{50}$ 84% $\frac{19}{100}$ 19%

$\frac{1}{4}$ 25% $\frac{65}{100}$ 65% $\frac{28}{50}$ 56% $\frac{56}{100}$ 56%

$\frac{3}{4}$ 75% $\frac{41}{100}$ 41% $\frac{20}{50}$ 40% $\frac{45}{50}$ 90%

③ What is 25% of each amount?

40p 10p   60cm 15cm   £4 £1   52g 13g

④ What is 40% of each amount?

£2 80p   80cm 32cm   £5 £2   10m 4m

⑤ Mary bakes a pie for tea. She eats a quarter ($\frac{1}{4}$), serves three-tenths ($\frac{3}{10}$) to her husband and divides the rest equally between her 3 children. What percentage of the pie does each child get?

15%

⑥ Circle the fractions which are the same as 60%.

$\boxed{\frac{3}{5}}$ $\frac{18}{20}$ $\boxed{\frac{30}{50}}$ $\boxed{\frac{90}{150}}$ $\frac{60}{90}$ $\frac{40}{70}$

⑦ Write four fractions which are the same as 30%. Answers may vary.

$\frac{3}{10}$ $\frac{30}{100}$ $\frac{6}{20}$ $\frac{9}{30}$

Recognising simple percentages, such as 50%, should be simple and understood quickly. Your child needs to realise the connection between fractions and percentages, especially those fractions relating to hundredths, tenths and fifths. If your child realises one penny is 1% of one pound, it will be very useful.

62 **63**

① Write each fraction as a percentage.

$\frac{7}{10}$ 70% $\frac{3}{5}$ 60% $\frac{3}{4}$ 75% $\frac{9}{10}$ 90%

② Increase each amount by $\frac{7}{10}$.

600 km 1 020 km   12 l 20.4 l   18 m 30.6 m   £4 £6.80

③ How much is 30% of each amount?

£2.50 75p   7 km 2.1 km   50 km 15 km   80p 24p

④ How much is 90% of each amount?

7 mm 6.3 mm   14 m 12.6 m   £6 £5.40   80p 72p

⑤ Increase each amount by 25%.

1 800 km 2 250 km   13 m 16.25 m   26 mm 32.5 mm   £18 £22.50

⑥ Reduce each amount by 20%.

7 000 km 5 600 km   £7.50 £6   6.5 m 5.2 m   2.8 cm 2.24 cm

⑦ Circle the fractions that are equivalent to 12.5%.

$\boxed{\frac{1}{8}}$ $\frac{3}{16}$ $\frac{5}{12}$ $\boxed{\frac{3}{24}}$ $\frac{2}{4}$

⑧ Circle the fractions that are larger than 60%.

$\frac{2}{5}$ $\boxed{\frac{4}{5}}$ $\boxed{\frac{7}{10}}$ $\boxed{\frac{3}{4}}$ $\frac{3}{10}$

⑨ A TV costs £350 but is reduced by 15% in a sale. How much will it cost in the sale?

£297.50

⑩ Petrol costs 130p per litre. How much will a litre of petrol cost if the price is increased by 10%?

143p

This work builds on the relationship between percentages and fractions. By now, your child should be able to recognise many fractions and their percentage equivalents, work successfully with both forms and convert easily between them.

Answers:

20–21 Beat the clock 1
40–41 Beat the clock 2
64–65 Beat the clock 3

These "Beat the clock" pages test your child's ability to quickly recall the lessons learned. The tests require your child to work under some pressure. As with most tests of this type, tell your child before he or she starts not to get stuck on one question, but to move on and return to the tricky one later if time allows. Encourage your child to record his or her score and the time taken to complete the test. You can also encourage your child to retake the test later to see if he or she can improve on his or her previous attempt.

20 / **21**

(1) 3	(2) 6	(3) 10	(31) 20 g	(32) 8 p	(33) 2 g
(4) 9	(5) 20	(6) 50	(34) 6 g	(35) 10 cm	(36) 16 g
(7) 1	(8) 5	(9) 40	(37) 40 p	(38) 12 m	(39) 22 g
(10) 15	(11) 25	(12) 6	(40) 4 p	(41) 14 cm	(42) 18 p
(13) 1 p	(14) 5 cm	(15) 10 m	(43) 12 p	(44) 18 g	(45) 3 cm
(16) 2 cm	(17) 3 cm	(18) 20 p	(46) 9 g	(47) 30 g	(48) 6 p
(19) 4 cm	(20) 6 g	(21) 9 m	(49) 21 m	(50) 27 cm	(51) 24 p
(22) 7 g	(23) 11 p	(24) 15 p	(52) 45 cm	(53) 15 g	(54) £33
(25) 10 p	(26) 4 g	(27) 1 cm	(55) 9 p	(56) 24 g	(57) £15
(28) 9 m	(29) 7 cm	(30) 20 g	(58) 36 m	(59) £3	(60) 21 g

40 / **41**

(1) $\frac{7}{2}$	(2) $\frac{22}{3}$	(3) $\frac{29}{10}$	(28) $\frac{4}{5}$	(29) $\frac{9}{10}$	(30) $\frac{3}{5}$
(4) $\frac{32}{7}$	(5) $\frac{26}{3}$	(6) $\frac{51}{12}$	(31) 12	(32) 5	(33) 8
(7) $\frac{21}{5}$	(8) $\frac{42}{5}$	(9) $\frac{53}{5}$	(34) 7	(35) 4	(36) 6
(10) $\frac{46}{7}$	(11) $\frac{60}{9}$	(12) $\frac{51}{5}$	(37) 9	(38) 40	(39) 100
(13) $\frac{41}{9}$	(14) $\frac{88}{9}$	(15) $\frac{125}{6}$	(40) 3	(41) 2	(42) $1\frac{1}{5}$
(16) $3\frac{7}{12}$	(17) $3\frac{3}{5}$	(18) $10\frac{1}{2}$	(43) $\frac{3}{5}$	(44) $10\frac{1}{5}$	(45) $10\frac{1}{2}$
(19) $3\frac{3}{10}$	(20) $4\frac{2}{3}$	(21) $6\frac{2}{8}$	(46) $\frac{3}{4}$	(47) $\frac{14}{8}$	(48) $\frac{10}{3}$
(22) $7\frac{1}{6}$	(23) $6\frac{1}{12}$	(24) $6\frac{1}{9}$	(49) $2\frac{5}{9}$	(50) $\frac{19}{4}$	(51) $\frac{90}{10}$
(25) $\frac{1}{2}$	(26) $\frac{2}{3}$	(27) $\frac{3}{4}$	(52) $\frac{120}{12}$	(53) $1\frac{2}{9}$	(54) $\frac{20}{6}$

64 / **65**

(1) $\frac{1}{4}$	(2) $\frac{3}{5}$	(3) $\frac{3}{4}$	(31) 0.5	(32) 0.25	(33) 0.75
(4) $\frac{1}{10}$	(5) $\frac{7}{20}$	(6) $\frac{17}{20}$	(34) 0.4	(35) 0.7	(36) 0.6
(7) $\frac{1}{2}$	(8) $\frac{9}{10}$	(9) $\frac{13}{20}$	(37) 0.3	(38) 0.8	(39) 0.1
(10) $\frac{3}{10}$	(11) $\frac{7}{10}$	(12) $\frac{1}{5}$	(40) 0.2	(41) 0.5	(42) 0.6
(13) $\frac{2}{5}$	(14) $\frac{1}{100}$	(15) $\frac{1}{20}$	(43) $\frac{1}{2}$	(44) $\frac{2}{5}$	(45) $\frac{4}{5}$
(16) $\frac{3}{4}$	(17) $\frac{1}{9}$	(18) $\frac{4}{10}$	(46) $\frac{17}{19}$	(47) $\frac{2}{3}$	(48) $\frac{1}{3}$
(19) $\frac{2}{3}$	(20) $\frac{5}{8}$	(21) $\frac{2}{9}$	(49) $\frac{4}{5}$	(50) $\frac{3}{5}$	(51) $\frac{1}{3}$
(22) $\frac{1}{3}$	(23) $\frac{2}{5}$	(24) $\frac{6}{35}$	(52) $\frac{2}{5}$	(53) $\frac{1}{4}$	(54) $\frac{2}{3}$
(25) $\frac{11}{12}$	(26) $\frac{1}{2}$	(27) $7\frac{1}{2}$	(55) $\frac{1}{3}$	(56) $\frac{9}{20}$	(57) $\frac{9}{14}$
(28) $\frac{9}{10}$	(29) $\frac{2}{3}$	(30) 17	(58) $\frac{1}{4}$	(59) $\frac{1}{10}$	(60) $\frac{1}{3}$